FIRE IN
THE HOLE

Sermons for Pentecost [Middle Third]
Cycle C Gospel Texts

BY W. ROBERT McCLELLAND

C.S.S Publishing Co., Inc.
Lima, Ohio

FIRE IN THE HOLE

Library of Congress Cataloging-in-Publication Data
McClelland, W. Robert (William Robert), 1931-
    Fire in the hole — sermons for Pentecost (Middle Third), Cycle C gospel texts / W. Robert McClelland.
        p.   cm.
    ISBN 1-55673-315-1
    1.   Pentecost season — Sermons.   2.   Sermons, American.
3.   Presbyterian Church — Sermon.   I.   Title.
BV4300.5.M33   1991
252'.6—dc20
                                                                91-3311
                                                                CIP

9136 / ISBN 1-55673-315-1   PRINTED IN U.S

Dedicated to my mentors in the venerable art of preaching: Edwin K. Roberts, at whose feet I discovered the relevancy of proclamation; George M. Gibson, in whose classes I learned the craft of homiletics; and Charles W. McClelland, with whom, in partnership, I found such joy in preaching.

Table Of Contents

C — Common Lectionary (Proper)
L — Lutheran Lectionary (Pentecost)
RC — Roman Catholic Lectionary (Ordinary Time)

Introduction

It seems to me that common charity demands some words of warning be spoken about the workings of the Spirit when entering the season of Pentecost. I, for one, am struck by the fact that our prayers opening church meetings at national and local levels asking for the Spirit's presence, are either born of ignorance or reckless fits of insanity. We pray as if we knew what we were doing. Have we forgotten the gale force winds with which the Holy Spirit blows? Just ask the survivors of Pentecost. The new wine simply cannot be contained in old wineskins. It always rips them apart. Therefore, if we insist on inviting the Spirit to grace our solemn assemblies we had best be prepared to stand back. Annie Dillard speaks of the "professionalism" with which we, as church leaders, sometimes approach God.

> *I often think of the set of pieces of liturgy as certain words which people have successfully addressed to God without getting killed. In the high churches they saunter through the liturgy like Mohawks along a strand of scaffolding who have long since forgotten their danger. If God were to blast such a service to bits, the congregation would be, I believe, genuinely shocked.*[1]

Not only the congregation! I believe we clergy, who usually do the praying at these affairs, would not know what to do if the Spirit did show up. The long season of Pentecost — the longest of all the seasons in the church year — affords us plenty of time to reflect on the fact that the dove of the Holy Spirit is not a tame pigeon. When the Spirit enters the sanctuary of the Lord, she comes with a whirlwind that blows the order of service out the window, scatters our well-prepared sermon notes, and rearranges our lives. The house of the Lord, it seems, is built on a cleft in the earth's crust that keeps shifting. God apparently loves earthquakes. Instead of a welcome mat spread at the door, perhaps we should post a sign that reads, "Danger! Enter at your own risk!"

One summer when I was in college, I got a job working with a railroad track gang. It was a hot job and hard, back breaking work, but it yielded a great suntan and promised status in the fall when I returned to the campus. We were building a railroad trestle which required blasting away the rock from a hillside so track could be laid. Holes were drilled in the rock. Sticks of dynamite were packed in the holes and ignition wires connected. It was always an exciting time. Tension mounted and hearts beat faster. When everything was ready for the blast, we took cover and the foreman yelled, "Fire in the hole!" We held our breath. The hillside erupted. The ground heaved beneath our feet. The earth trembled. And when the dust cleared, we could see that the landscape had been changed.

We dare not forget that fire — the Fire of the Spirit — is the abiding symbol of Pentecost. To be set ablaze with fingers of fire, as were the early disciples, is to discover that some things are apt to be incinerated; old ideas that feel comfortable, settled dogma that removes the mystery of the Holy, theological answers that silence searching questions.

This, then, is a book of homiletical musings following the suggested lectionary texts for the season of Pentecost. I take it that the art of preaching during this season is to get close enough to these texts to see them sputter with dangerous potential and then run for our lives, yelling, "Fire in the hole!"

W. Robert McClelland
St. Louis, 1991

The Politics Of Love

Luke sets the familiar parable of the good Samaritan in the context of two commands: Love God and neighbor; and Go, do likewise! Furthermore, it is clear that by casting the parable with Jewish bad guys and a Samaritan good guy, Jesus wants our love to transcend ideological differences and respond to human suffering and injustice wherever it may be found.

Christian spirituality has always been characterized by its loving concern for others, but it has had trouble seeing the political dimensions of its love. In its focus on heaven it has approached the ills of this world with a first aid kit when major surgery was required. It has had difficulty seeing that the wounds needing treatment are inflicted by the political and economic structures of a society. One denomination official put it, "Local communities, churches, and judicatories have hunger programs that place an inordinate emphasis upon fast days, gleaners' groups, and food distribution programs which emphasize direct food relief, and then frequently ignore the necessity of dealing with systematic change and the fundamental causes of hunger and malnutrition."

There is a crucial distinction to be made between personal acts of love that aim to feed the poor, and political actions which seek to remedy the root causes of poverty. Of course, feeding the poor is required of us; as is offering a cup of water to the thirsty, clothing the naked, and visiting the prisoner. But we live in a world where political systems contribute to an economic stratification in which the rich get richer and the poor get poorer. The lack of educational opportunities, lingering racism, inequality of taxation; all contribute to the complex malaise of poverty. Personal acts of love may salve

9

consciences but they leave the disease untreated. A piety that cultivates personal virtues such as love and sensitivity to the needs of others — without addressing the societal causes of human suffering — fosters counterfeit love. Loving our neighbor forces us into the political arena where the decisions effecting the lives of people are made. Love must be spelled out politically and economically if we we are to carry out the biblical mandate to love God and our neighbor.

When Jesus spoke in his hometown synagogue he began his sermon to the local gentry by quoting the Old Testament prophet Isaiah, "The Spirit of the Lord is upon me, because he has anointed me to preach good news to the poor. He has sent me to proclaim release to the captives and recovering of sight to the blind, to set at liberty those who are oppressed, to proclaim the acceptable year of the Lord (Luke 4:18, 19)." His speech sounds strangely like that of a political candidate running for office, especially since he claimed that the promise was as good as fulfilled by his presence among them. But by doing so, Jesus nailed down one of the central planks to God's political platform.

In both the Old and New Testaments God is portrayed as the champion of orphans and widows, the maimed and the sick, captives and aliens. Scripture reveals the Divine bias for all those who yearn for a place in the sun and who can never find it. They have been crowded out and forgotten by those who already have a deep tan. To view the world through the eyes of Christ, as we are called to do, we must acknowledge, understand, and accept responsibility for our connectedness to each other in the human family.

This is not an abstract principle that Jesus puts before us. It is as concrete as our neighbor in need. We could paraphrase Jesus' words without doing mischief to his intent,
"I was hungry
and you cut my food stamps,
took away my school lunch,
dumped 'surplus' crops like oranges to rot rather
than let me eat them.

10

"I was thirsty
and you continued to let the acid rain kill the fish
in the lakes,
and allowed river water to become unfit to drink.
"I was a stranger without a home
and you wiped out the subsidies which were my only
hope for a decent place to live.
"I was naked
and you cut my welfare check so much that I could
not buy clothes,
you wiped out the community service agencies that
were helping me,
the job-training programs that gave me some chance
of supporting myself,
the day care centers which allowed me to work while
my children received good care;
you refused to provide an adequate minimum wage
so that I can't afford to work anyway.
"I was sick
and you capped Medicaid so that I was turned away
from the hospital.
"I was in prison
and you wiped out the legal services, so that 'equal
justice under law' became a mockery.
You took away the lawyer helping my family avoid
eviction by a condo developer.
"You did all this and more, you said, to save your
economy and balance your budget.
But the money you had been spending to help me
you added to your spending for implements of war.
"And you cut the taxes of the affluent so they would
have even more while I would have even less."
Then Americans will answer,
"Lord, when did we see you hungry, or thirsty, or
a stranger, or naked, or sick, or in prison, and would
not help you?"

The Lord will reply,

"I tell you, whenever you refused to help one of the least important ones, you refused to help me."[2]

By telling the story of the Samaritan's love, Jesus shows us that to love the least important ones is to love God. The obligation to love God and others is given urgency by the one command, "Go, and do likewise!" To love the neighbor — that is, those who are the victims of oppression and injustice — is to love God. Our love of God is not measured by the orthodoxy of our beliefs or the earnestness of our praise. It is, rather, gauged by our restoration to wholeness those who have been oppressed. In our society that kind of love is inescapably political.

Most people are of the opinion that politics and religion do not mix, or at least ought not mix and, consequently, it is one of those taboo topics in the church. The belief trails a long history. I imagine the Pharaoh of vintage Egypt did not appreciate Moses coming to court with his impudent demand, "Let my people go!" He must have been a firm advocate of the separation of church and state, no doubt because to grant the demand, would have disrupted the economy of the nation. Nevertheless, Moses was there because of a Holy calling.

I mean to suggest that a biblical faith requires of us a mixture of religion and politics because it sees God's creation as a work of Divine love. Law is the political means by which we, in groups, respond to God's creative initiative to love our neighbors and care for our planet. To love in the way that God has loved us is to work toward a time when the law of the land reflects the Divine intention for the world.

The political groups of which we are unavoidably a part make decisions about those whom Jesus calls, "neighbors." These decisions are called public policy. People live and die because of them. As members of society and citizens of God's kingdom, we have a special obligation to participate actively in making these decisions of public policy.

Because the church is not a homogeneous group of people who see things eye to eye or who understand God's will in the same way, it will always be a place of lively discussion of diverse views as we try to discover what is God's will. To paraphrase James Gustafson's observation; the church is not a place of religious, much less political, agreement. It is, rather, a place of religious and political discussion in the light of Scripture. To short circuit this discussion by quoting a few isolated verses from the Bible is not only inadequate, but woefully naive. Scriptural proof-texts cannot be applied to our time as though no water has flowed under the historical bridge.

The issue of drinking, for example, is complicated, not only because of the modern technology of distillation which increases the alcoholic content of beverages, but the invention of the automobile. In the days of Jesus, a pedestrian had considerable time to get out of the way of a drunken ox cart driver. Today, travel is vastly different as are the issues involved. They do not lend themselves to the advice of writers for whom speeding automobiles and souped-up horsepower did not exist even in their wildest flights of imagination.

What does it mean to love my neighbor in a labor-management negotiation over wages and working conditions? Who is my neighbor? Is it the person across the bargaining table from me or is it those whom I represent and to whom I am responsible? What would Jesus do in such a situation? I must confess, I do not know and neither does anyone else. The Bible never envisioned big business much less labor unions.

We will, therefore, be left to our own best judgment about the question. We must risk some answer, but it will be a risk of faith and no doubt other Christians will see the matter differently. Hopefully we will make our decisions in the best light of our faith at the time, and not cop out by compartmentalizing it into worlds of the sacred and the secular; never the twain to meet. We can expect that when politics and religion mix in the arena of faith, as indeed they must, emotions will be ignited and people will get involved. But no one will be bored — a condition sadly present in many churches today. Religious discourse will be heated because it will matter. It will be relevant and carry consequences.

For those who want a biblical precedent for such a model of the church, let me suggest the motley group of disciples. There, following Jesus along the dusty roads of Galilee, was Matthew, the tax collector. His income was dependent upon retaining the Roman political party in power. He was a company man and voted a straight ticket. There, too, was Simon the Zealot, trudging side by side with Matthew on those hot dusty roads. Like Matthew he was also a disciple of Jesus. But his political persuasion led him to become a terrorist. Zealots were dedicated to the violent resistance of Roman oppression including the overthrow of the government. On any normal day, or dark night, Simon would have slipped a knife between the ribs of Matthew the tax collector, and done it to the glory of God! And Matthew would have turned Simon in to the authorities as a revolutionary. Yet there they were. Both of them. Side by side. Disciples of Jesus, not because they agreed with one another, but because they were both seeking to be obedient to the calling of discipleship. What is fascinating is that there is not a shred of evidence to suggest that either of them changed their political views. Assumptions to the contrary bring unwarranted presuppositions to the text. That which bound them together was not agreement about religion or politics but the fact that each of them, in his own way, was following Jesus. Which, in turn, meant they had to trust one another's faith and ethics even though they did not agree with either. Imagine the heated arguments they must have had as they walked and talked together! Never a dull moment!

The trouble with most churches today is that there is no evidence of that kind of diversity. Many church leaders, not to mention their constituents, find any difference of opinion, and certainly conflict, to be very threatening. They seek to avoid it at all costs, either by denying it or burying it. Consequently we have successfully screened out the differences or suppressed them in the name of peace and unity. The result is counterfeit love because it lacks political dimension.

The point to be gained is crucial. The unity of the church is not found in the oneness of our agreement — political or religious — but in our common allegiance to Jesus Christ. That which binds us together as a community of faith is our common desire to be obedient to God's will which as Luke reminds us is to love our neighbor — and do it now!

Christian faith is on trial in the eyes of the world. It looks at the church to see if we put our practice where our proclamation is. Our claim is that God was in Christ reconciling the world. Not merely forgiving it; reconciling it. Forgiveness moves in the direction of the righteous to the sinner and, thereby, maintains in many subtle ways the distinctions and the rifts between them. Reconciliation, on the other hand, is accomplished when equals who differ are able to accept, though not necessarily agree with, one another.

What usually happens in human relations, and certainly church relations, is not reconciliation in the midst of differences but the elimination of all differences. Not conflict managed creatively, but conflict denied. Churches either do not allow conflict; screening out certain practices, people, or beliefs, or they pretend that there are no differences and call themselves a fellowship of love simply because disagreements are not taken seriously. In neither case is reconciliation practiced. Because believers are not encouraged to disagree they do not know what to do with their differences. They become frustrated because they feel their views are not valued. They discover there is no room for them in the community of believers and tend to become bitter because they are not part of the power structure which successfully imposes its will on everyone else. As a result the differences go underground where they work as a cancer sapping the energy of the community of faith or erupt in open schism. Or they drop out altogether. Or they start another denomination.

If the church cannot demonstrate the reconciling power of Christ to the world, it will never be able to convince the world that it has any good news to offer. The world with all of its pluralism of perspectives and variety of viewpoints, will not be impressed by anything the church has to say as long as it sees simply another group of homogeneous people who enjoy

15

scratching one another's backs. There are plenty of groups for bright bridge players or happy hymn singers.

But if the world sees a lively discussion of differences taking place within a fellowship of love, where the discipline of trust carries across the abyss of disagreement, it may take a second look. If the world sees the Word that in Christ there is neither Jew nor Greek, Democrat nor Republican — sees that Word become flesh, it just may be convinced that there is something to this faith that we profess.

The church is a community of faith practicing godly love. We are called to be lovers. Christians do not leave their politics at the door of the church as they enter because the church is that group of Republicans and Democrats, liberals and conservatives who is learning to be good Samaritans and love our neighbors in need.

Mary Has Chosen The Good Portion

The Genesis creation narrative tells us that God created the world, and all that is in it, in six short days, a remarkable burst of energy even for God. Understandably, God was tired — an idea which has eluded learned theologians — but the author of the story insists that, ". . . on the seventh day God finished his work which he had done and he rested on the seventh day from all his work . . . So God blessed the seventh day and hallowed it, because on it God rested from all his work which he had done in creation (Genesis 2:2, 3)." Written on the first page of our Bibles and woven into the fabric of the universe is the divine provision for leisure time. The black preacher's prayer falls on a sympathetic ear, "Slow me down, Lord. I'm goin' too fast. I can't see my brother when he's walking past. I miss a lot of things day by day when it comes my way. Slow me down, Lord, I'm goin' too fast."

Yet, slowing down and taking time off is just what we find so hard to do. We can easily empathize with Martha's plea, "Tell Mary to get off her duff and give me a hand." Preparing dinner for so distinguished a guest was worthy work. Clearly, Mary was goofing off. Our knee jerk assessment, therefore, renders the verdict, "That's not fair. Mary was shirking her responsibility and making more work for poor Martha. She was being thoughtless and self-centered. It wasn't very 'Christian' of her." Consequently, we are genuinely surprised and truly affronted when Jesus reprimands Martha, not Mary, and insists that Mary has, in fact, chosen the good portion.

Martha's complaint from the kitchen reflects the commonly held assumption in religious circles that work is more godly

17

than leisure. The young John Wesley is reported to have boasted, "Leisure and I have parted company." Indeed, our entire society views work as a virtue. The American free enterprise system is built on the assumption that work is the central purpose of life. To work is to be somebody. Apart from our work we don't know who we are or what our worth is. Not to work is to be a cipher on the page of society's reckoning. I recently talked with a person who wanted to work with people. I suggested that perhaps some kind of volunteer activity might fulfill her need. But she said, "No. Working as a volunteer doesn't carry the same satisfaction or status that a paid job does." Doing something for nothing — even though we enjoy doing it — doesn't count for much in our eyes or that of society's. We need to be paid for it. The need runs deep in our psyche.

Most of us grow into adulthood with a poor self image. We do not like ourselves very much, so we have a compulsive need to earn our worth. Work is assumed to be the source of our identity and worth. The person who enjoys work may be even worse off than the person who finds it dull and tiresome because the tendency is to make work an all consuming passion. Some of us, literally, work ourselves to death trying to prove our value. A workaholic minister friend of mine delayed needed by-pass surgery until his vacation just so he could continue working; doing those "necessary things," without which his church and the kingdom could not survive. I suspect if he had died of a heart attack while in the pulpit he would have been regarded by his congregation and community as a Christian martyr. I suspect Jesus might have thought him a fool.

In any case, if work is the way by which we gain worth, then idleness is to be avoided. Extended leisure is not only the enemy of our capitalistic system but individual worth as well.

Ironically the whole goal of American industry is to produce more goods and services more efficiently and economically so that eventually we can eliminate jobs or spend fewer hours at them. Some surveys estimate that by the end of this century we will have a 20-hour work week. We are in the business of producing leisure. Unfortunately, leisure means time to think or worse: to feel. Studies indicate that many men and women seek moonlighting jobs not for economic reasons but to escape boredom.

Leisure, therefore, raises the identity question. As leisure time increases we may expect depression and anxiety to rise along with the incidence of attempts to escape such as drinking and doing drugs, suicide and crime. Extended leisure such as illness or retirement can be devastating and even fatal. A former parishioner dreaded retirement and was ill prepared for it. When the time came he didn't know what to do with himself. Gradually he underwent a change of personality. He disintegrated mentally as well as physically and soon died in a nursing home. His identity was tied up in his work.

Even vacation leisure time can be a problem for those addicted to work. One summer another couple joined my wife and I for a week at the lake in Minnesota. We had not been there 24 hours before our farmer friend was worrying about the corn back home. The weeds might be infesting his fields. His neighbors might be saying he was lazy. For him, the vacation was a bust. He and his wife went home three days early. He could not stand idle time.

So, along with Martha, we ride off into the sunset, singing, "Hi Ho! Hi Ho! It's off to work we go . . ."

Some time ago a friend of mine came to me with the exciting news that he had just received a job promotion. He said it would mean professional advancement and a sizable increase in salary. Unfortunately, it meant leaving the community. "My family doesn't want to leave," he lamented. "We simply hate to leave our friends here, and the church which has meant so much to us. The whole thing is tearing the children apart."

As his pastor, I found myself reassuring him by saying "The kids will get over that. Children adjust very well. After all, that's a normal part of life."

Later, when I had a chance to reflect on our conversation, I wondered why we both had assumed that a promotion should be accepted when it is offered, even though it means tearing up spiritual and social roots? Is such dislocation to be expected, and accepted, as a normal part of life? It is precisely that assumption which is called in question by Jesus' reply to Martha.

One-fifth of our nation's population moves every year. This means, theoretically, that all of us can expect to move once every five years. If we do not move that often, someone is moving even more frequently to average out the statistics. Many of us have, in fact, moved within the last five years, and therefore, can remember the trauma such moves caused our families when we had to leave dear friends behind. Frequent moving has, among other effects, the unfortunate result of making relative that most important of human values, human relationships.

That we find new friends in our new location is a gift of God's grace. But notice, it is God's grace, not the company's. The company gets no credit for this gift, nor does it offer it. The system asks, indeed, demands, that we sacrifice human relationship for its sake. People are simply functions who fit into it and make the system work more effectively.

The subtlety of this self-interest appears when a business hires a person. It first develops a job description. The job description defines the function that a person will fulfill in the corporate structure. The company does not hire a person. It hires a complex of talents, abilities, and skills to fit the job description which, in turn, makes the system operate more smoothly. The system cares only about itself and its self-perpetuation.

When we put the matter this way, we can see that there is something slightly hypocritical about the benevolent P. R. that would have us believe the company has our best interests at heart. It justifies itself because it makes a better brand of aspirin to relieve our headaches, or produces better shoes so we can live more comfortably, or develops a better deodorant so we can enjoy one another's company.

Of course, the company wants us to be happy and fulfilled people. After all, happy and fulfilled people are contented workers. Orwellian experiments have been carried out in which tiny electrodes were implanted in the brains of rabbits. By pressing a lever the rabbit could cause a minuscule amount of electricity to flow to its brain activating the so-called pleasure areas. The rabbits became so addicted to the self-induced pleasure that they seemed to live for nothing else. Happy rabbits and contented workers do not seek to escape the system. They do just what the system wants. Promotions, benefits, and salary increases are the carrots held out to workers so that we will produce more, contentedly, and loyally. And the carrots work as incentives because they bring pleasure and a sense of worth.

Brazilian theologian, Rubem Alves, suggests that we imagine ourselves locked in a room with no windows or doors. No matter how nice the room is furnished we will very quickly become bored and suffer claustrophobia. Inevitably we will begin to probe the walls and floor, looking for a way of escape. Then, Alves suggests, that we imagine ourselves in a castle with a thousand and one luxurious rooms, filled with surprises and pleasures. As we tire of one room we can move to the next, and the next, indefinitely exploring the castle. So absorbed are we in our search that we never notice that the castle, like the other room, has neither windows nor doors. We are equally a prisoner but it never occurs to us to escape.

Enslavement is the issue. And Martha was trapped in her virtuous castle of work fixing dinner for Jesus. Yet, it is Jesus who says the idle Mary has chosen the better part.

Every institution, whether it be government, business, or the church, develops a system to secure its own interests and survival. The extent to which a system will go to survive becomes shockingly evident if we remember the Watergate affair and the more recent attempts to cover up the illegal sale of arms to Nicaraguan contras. In both of these, any means — criminal or otherwise — were justified in order to perpetuate the system and guarantee its survival.

Similarly, the buck-passing and legal maneuvering employed by companies guilty of spilling oil, dumping toxic chemicals, spouting air pollutants, and over-cutting timber remind us that the modern corporation is not, and cannot be expected to be, a responsible institution in our society. For all of the self-congratulatory handouts depicting the large firm as a good citizen, the fact remains that a business exists purely and simply to make more profits, a large proportion of which it proceeds to pour back into itself.

Such an indictment may be worded more harshly than we would like to hear. But I know of no company that takes pride in submitting an annual report to its shareholders revealing mere business as usual. Each year it strives to show an increase in sales and profits. Businesses are self-serving. Despite the claim of a fast food chain that they do it all for us, the fact is that if doing it for us did not prove profitable they would change their motto and their policy.

The point to be grasped is not that business is bad or work is evil. The point is simply that those means for getting ahead provided by the company are not designed with our well-being in mind. They are designed with the system's good in mind; its survival and growth.

Mary chose to turn her back on the system. She chose to leave Martha with all those pots and pans in the kitchen in order to sit at the feet of Jesus and listen to him. He had a lot to say about life and its meaning. He shared his thoughts, without remuneration or enslavement to a publishing deadline, with anyone not too busy to listen.

It is surprising how often the Bible commends those who take time off to wait for the Lord. "They who wait for the Lord," says Isaiah, "shall renew their strength. They shall mount up with wings like eagles. They shall run and not be weary. They shall walk and not faint (40:31)." In Jesus' eyes, work was not the fountain of life. Therefore, it could wait for more important matters. He was not, as the phrase diplomatically puts it, gainfully employed. Others, less diplomatic, might have said he was irresponsible and lacked ambition; a parasite on the human race — dawdling away his time on the hillsides with cronies, playing with children, talking about birds and flowers — instead of helping out in the family carpentry shop. Clearly, if Jesus had been born in our time he would never have been offered a promotion by his employers. He was not on a career track.

What ought to disturb us is that our faith calls this man Savior. He who did not fit in is called Savior. He who did not sacrifice anything to get ahead is called Savior. He who took time to consider the lilies of the field and the birds of the air is called Savior. He who enjoyed living and spoke of its abundance is called Savior.

Why? Because he forgives our sins? Yes! But more important for our thinking here, he saves us from the authoritative claims of the system that says sacrificing our humanity for the sake of the system is the normal way of life. The system that expects us to fit in and go with the flow because that's the way it is.

Jesus is our Savior because he offers us an alternative. When Jesus was tired, he got away from people and took a rest. He took his vacations when he needed them, not when the company said he could. He left some of the pressing crowd unhealed, untaught. When Jesus saw children he gathered them around him. When people wanted to talk, he took the time to listen. The machinery of production ground to a halt because he believed we do not live by bread and paychecks alone. And he justified all of his actions by saying, "This is my Father's business!" Mary too had chosen the good portion.

Jesus is the Christ because he demonstrates a lifestyle that saves us from the system which would have us believe fitting in is more important than living. To call Jesus "Savior," is both revolutionary and liberating because to call him "Savior," is to say that his set of values is the divine definition of what is really important in life.

And — he was crucified because he did not fit into the system. It was the system that demanded his death; Pilate on hand to speak for the government, the high priest representing the interests of religion, the temple moneychangers speaking for the business tycoons. All of them wanted this threat removed from their midst. The crucifixion is the grating reminder that the systems to which we so easily give our allegiance are locked in a life and death struggle with him who represents Life.

The other day I was in an office building and saw an interesting bit of life take place in front of my eyes. A woman came into the office to talk to her husband who was sitting behind his desk. When she finished and was about to leave, she leaned over to kiss him good-bye. Nervously, he looked around and brushed her aside. He said it would not be appropriate to kiss her there. His perception of what was appropriate in his working environment disallowed him to relate to the person he loved most in life.

The crucifixion reminds us that the system and Life sometimes come at each other from opposite sides of the ring. The resurrection represents God's permission to say "No!" to the system's demands. The resurrection is God's vindication of Christ's values. We do not live by bread alone but by every word that proceeds from the mouth of God. Mary sat leisurely listening. And Jesus said, "Mary has chosen the good portion."

Let Us Pray!

In James Baldwin's *Blues For Mister Charlie*, there is an arresting scene in which a young boy announces before his grandmother and the world that he no longer believes in God. The wise and unperturbed woman replies, "Ain't no way you can't believe in God, boy. You just try holding your breath long enough to die."

No less than breathing or the sucking of a newborn infant, prayer is instinctive human behavior. The disciples' plea, "Lord, teach us to pray," arises from a primal urge deep within the human psyche. During World War II it was a cliche that there were no atheists in foxholes. Deep calls to deep. Spirit seeks spirit. Speaking autobiographically, Augustine observed, "Our souls are restless until they find their rest in thee, O God." A contemporary commentator put it simply, "There is a God-shaped space in each of us that seeks its own filling."

Nevertheless, for many of us, practicing prayer is like traveling to a foreign country. We go there occasionally, but we go as tourists. And like most tourists we feel uncomfortable and out of place. So we move on before too long and go elsewhere.

Of course, most of us would agree that prayer is a proven technique for bringing peace of mind in time of trouble. No doubt some of us could cite wonders accomplished by the power of prayer. I know of one little boy, near and dear to my heart, who had such faith in the efficacy of divine intervention that he prayed, "Lord, make me a good boy; and if at first you don't succeed, try, try, again."

But Jesus does not present prayer as a hot line to God, used only in cases of emergency. He does not require that we bow our heads, close our eyes, or fold our hands. He does not even

25

demand that we end our prayers with the liturgical phrase, "In Jesus' name. Amen." There may be nothing wrong with these prayer practices if they do not inhibit our coming to God comfortably; but they are not required by Jesus. What he does say, is that we are to come before the throne of grace boldly. Most of us, I suppose, have been taught that we ought to approach God humbly, with heads bowed and on bended knee. We learned that when we bring our requests to the throne of grace we are to add, "If it be your will," so as not to crowd God. After all, we don't want to appear arrogant, and we certainly do not want to offend the Almighty. It would be like biting the hand that feeds us. We come into God's presence as guests, therefore. We view prayer as a privilege, and we do not want to abuse it or take it lightly. So we come with hat in hand. We call it "humility."

Recently I was called to the hospital where a parishioner was terminally ill. The patient was a young widow; mother of two small children. After offering prayer for her recovery and a reunion with her family, I added the pious phrase, typically used in prayers of petition, ". . . If it be your will." Later, I reflected on my visit, and particularly those words in my prayer. "Of course God's will for her is wholeness and health," I thought to myself. "God is the creator of life and wills joy and health for all of us. And clearly those children need their mother."

Suddenly, I realized my words — if it be God's will — were not proper theological protocol so much as fear that God could not heal the woman. They offered God an escape clause.

Certainly, there is a time and place for turning things over to God's superior wisdom — ". . . nevertheless, not as I will, but as you will" — but the words do not appear in the model of prayer Jesus gave his disciples. We add them as a mark of our humility, but I suspect more often than not, "If it be your will . . ." are weasel words born of a failure of nerve rather than humility. The pious phrase gives God an out. It takes the Almighty off the hook as if the Lion of Judah needed rescuing by us. Rather than exhibiting humility it reveals the height of arrogance. We are trying to make God look good!

Our traditional understandings of prayer are curious at best, and misleading at worst, when we contrast them with some of the biblical models. A case in point is that robust conversation in the Old Testament between Abraham and God over the fate of Sodom, sister sin city of Gomorrah. He comes to God and haggles with the Almighty. No hint of shyness on his part. No false piety. Abraham says to God, "You don't mean to tell me, Lord, you're going to destroy a whole city just because a few of the folks have upset you. Suppose I find 50 who can pass the fitness test?" The Lord thinks it over, and decides he can live with the compromise. But Abraham, always the bargainer, sees that he has his foot in the door and warms to the challenge. He says, "Would you settle for 40? How about 30? Would you believe 10?"

Now, I do not for a minute want to suggest that prayer is a sure-fire technique for getting the things we desire. Indeed, one of the things that infuriates me most about radio and television faith healers is that they seem to imply if we would just pray more frequently, or more sincerely, or send them a bigger check, results would be guaranteed. No! God is not a cosmic bellhop who jumps because we ring the bell. Yet, clearly the story of Abraham dickering with God suggests that the options are open. The terms of life are negotiable, and it is possible that God's mind may be changed by virtue of our praying.

That may not sound like a traditional understanding of God, but textbook theology is not the issue here; relationship with the Divine is!

So back to the Lord's prayer! Jesus begins with the amazingly bold words, "Our Father . . ." As John Knox lay on his death-bed he began to pray the Lord's prayer. He didn't get very far, however. In fact he didn't get beyond these first two words, "Our Father . . ." Startled, he opened his eyes and looked at those standing beside his bed. "How can anyone pray those words?" he wondered.

It's a good question. How dare we assume so intimate a relationship with God Almighty? Only because Jesus teaches us to pray that way! In teaching us to pray, Jesus wants us to view prayer as a family affair. We are to come to God with the same confidence that we would approach a loving parent, certain that we are welcome and our desires are of genuine concern to God.

The way some of us approach God would lead objective observers to think we were approaching a tyrant who could take our head off. We come fawning on bended knee, hands folded and with eyes downcast. Today we would consider any parent who wanted us to crawl on our knees when we spoke to be abusive. Surely, God is at least as approachable as a loving, earthly parent.

The Bible gives us permission to call God, "Daddy!" The apostle Paul addressed God as "Abba! Father!" in Romans 8:15. "Abba," is the Aramaic word translated in the Greek as "pater" or "father," but in Aramaic, as "Daddy." It is the familiar, very personal term for father. Jesus invites us to come very intimately to God in prayer. We do not come in awe. We are not in the presence of a high potentate. This is a family matter. "When you pray say, 'Father!'" Not, "Our Father." And not, "Our Father who art in heaven," which is how Matthew recounts the Lord's Prayer. But Matthew is almost certainly reiterating a liturgical prayer of the early church in his gospel. Luke's version is probably the more accurate. "When you pray, say, 'Father!'" As such, it is an attention getter. "Father, are you listening? I have some things I want to say."

One of the amazing things in the model of prayer given to us by Jesus is that he teaches us to pray in the imperative mood! Sometimes we have trouble actually believing that Jesus teaches us to put demands before God rather than polite requests. But there they are in the Bible. Jesus offers a series of staccato, imperative commands; and says this is the way to pray! "Hallowed be Thy name! Thy Kingdom, come! Give us each our daily bread! Forgive us our sins! Lead us not into temptation!" We are to know what we want and to lay our requests before God with courage and conviction.

What is so surprising is that Jesus does not teach us to pray humbly. These are demands laid before the throne of Grace. Not, "if it be your will." Not, "pretty please, give us our daily bread." It is not a request. It is an imperative. "God! Give us bread!" The prayer is simply, just "Do it!"

Suddenly the defenders of the faith are right there taking a stance as if protecting the honor of God. With great indignation and self-righteousness they will protest, "Hold it, Rev! Hold it right there! That sounds a little pushy, don't you think? The way I was taught to pray required some humility. You didn't want to push God. You had no right to be there in the first place so you came on quietly and with a little flattery, like how great and good God is. You buttered up the divine Ego before asking any favors."

A minister friend of mine was in the habit of telling his little girl a bedtime story each evening before tucking her in for the night. One evening he told her such a thrilling tale her eyes popped open. She sat up in bed studying her father. "Daddy, do you mean it, or are you just preaching?" Sometimes it is hard to know with preachers. Sometimes it is even hard to know with Jesus.

But such boldness is again affirmed in the parable Jesus tells immediately following his instructions in prayer. A man awakens his friend at midnight with a request for food and is rebuffed. The man continues to bang on the door allowing his friend no sleep until he responds to his request. The friend responds for no other reason than to get rid of the nuisance at his door. Jesus concludes, "Ask, and it will be given you; seek, and you will find; knock, and it will be opened to you." It must have raised the eyebrows of his pious listeners because the clear point of the story seems to be that bold persistence pays off in matters of prayer.

Jesus' story of the prodigal son (Luke 15:11-32) amplifies the same point. The younger brother came to the father and demanded his share of the family inheritance. The father gave it to him without any argument, and off the lad went to seek his fortune. The loyal elder brother, on the other hand, stayed home and dutifully worked on the family farm. Understandably, when his younger brother returned home, having squandered half of the family's fortune, he complained about the welcome home celebration. "Father, you never gave me a feast. You never put a ring on my finger. You never threw a robe around my shoulders." But the father replies, "Son, all that I have is yours." The tragedy implied is that the elder brother never asked for anything from his father. He never availed himself of the "all that is mine is yours." He lived like a hired servant rather than a family member. He suffered a failure of nerve and as a result of neglected prayer he missed out on the big party.

In the things of prayer it appears to be, as it is with the things of life, that the world stands aside for those who have a plan. Prayer is a privilege, yes. But the way Jesus presents it, it is a privilege for the robust who come into the presence of God and approach the throne of grace with confidence, knowing what they want of Divine providence.

My daughter is a student in California. She keeps in close touch with the family. Not by writing letters, of course. She always calls long distance. Collect! She usually begins her conversations on the phone with, "Hey Dad, guess what!" The liturgy calls for the response, "What?" And then she will disclose the latest episode in her marvelous life adventure. She called the other evening. "Hey, Dad, guess what!" "What?" I said dutifully. "Over spring break all the kids are going to Hawaii. I'd like to go too. Can I? And will you spring for the air fare?" That was simple. I said, "No!" and we went on to other topics of conversation.

But what a model for prayer. She knew what she wanted. I heard very clearly her request. And I was able to say "No," just as clearly. How different the conversation might have been if she had said, "Dear Father, are you listening? I have a few things that I would like to talk over with you if you have the time. I know how much you have on your mind with all that you have to do and I really don't mean to intrude. But I know you have my best interests at heart and want me to get as broad an education as possible."

"For heaven's sake, get to the point!"

No wonder the Holy One dozes off during so many of our prayers. God is bored! Talking with my daughter is interesting conversation. She doesn't always get her way, but she is always a delight and her excitement and zest for life is contagious. Jesus wants us to be specific in our requests. In effect he says, "Know what you want and go for it."

God, of course, is always free to say, "No!" just as I did with my daughter's request to vacation in Hawaii. Prayer is not like rubbing a magic bottle to make the genie appear. God is not a bellhop who runs our errands or grants our every wish. But it is clear that the issues of life are open to discussion.

Look again at how the writers of the Old Testament tell the story of the Exodus and the events leading up to it (Exodus chapters 3 and 4). It is pivotal in the Pentateuch. Incredibly, Israel's faith was built on a story which featured God negotiating the terms of Moses' job description. We can forgive Moses his lack of enthusiasm for God's proposition as he makes first one excuse and then another since it puts him at great risk with the powers that be. Moses does not seem to be afflicted with a martyr complex. Therefore, God has to bargain collectively with Moses; certainly not a requirement for an omnipotent Sovereign who could dictate terms and demand unconditional surrender. To say that God limits his or her divine power is to beg the question and miss the point: God chooses to be our prayer Partner not as One characterized by omnipotence, but intimacy. We can only wonder what would have been the outcome if Moses had decided against being a servant of the Lord?

Clearly, Jesus does not present prayer as a relationship that has God on the end of a string like a marionette. But neither do the biblical models of prayer portray our prayer Partner as a puppeteer pulling our strings to make us dance, offering only the appearance of free choice. Scripture seems to suggest that life is an experience somewhat similar to that of playing chess with a Grand Master. The Master opens. We make our move. Again it is the Grand Master's turn. After some thought he makes his move . . . but only after we have made ours. Indeed, the game plan of the Grand Master is dependent upon our moves and can only be determined in response to them. There is, of course, no way we can defeat a Grand Master of chess. He is far too experienced for us. But how he wins cannot be known in advance because his moves cannot be predetermined. That is what keeps the game interesting; both for us and for the Grand Master.

This is why it makes sense to say, "Let us pray . . . ."

Proper 13
Pentecost 11
Ordinary Time 18
Luke 12:13-21

Sharing Shalom

The Bible has a great deal to say about wealth and the people who own it. This parable of Jesus for example: The usual interpretation speaks of it as a teaching concerning the folly of a life devoted to the accumulation of wealth. It is ridiculous to seek security through riches. The foolishness becomes obvious, so the interpretation goes, when suddenly one night the man dies and must stand before God. Then he sees with tragic clarity the utter folly of it all. It was stupid, if not sinful, to amass riches. Better, therefore, to be spiritually rich and economically poor.

The trouble with this traditional interpretation of the text is that it does not square with our experience. Many of us enjoy working. Some of us find great satisfaction and pleasure in the challenges and rewards of work. We do not find working, and the accumulation of those things which come as a result of our endeavors, to be an evil. Moreover, we have managed a good balance between work and leisure and enjoy the things that money can buy which do, in fact, bring us happiness.

The Old Testament calls this sense of happy well-being, "Shalom." I do not mean to suggest that people on welfare cannot find happiness. It is just that I do not wish to trade the problems of wealth for those of poverty and I know of few who do. Possessions do enhance our lives. Our experience leads us to conclude that money has the ability to bring blessings to ourselves and others. It has, in short, the power to convey God's Shalom.

Because our experience does not square with the traditional understanding of Jesus' parable, we fail to take it seriously.

We manage to feel guilty, of course, because most of us are affluent by this world's standards and assume the bony finger of accusation is pointed at us by Jesus, but we do not really believe that riches are evil or the satisfaction that we derive from our work is blasphemous. Consequently, when we give money to the church or charitable causes we do so dutifully, perhaps grudgingly; out of a sense of obligation and guilt.

Our failure to take the parable seriously, however, may not be an indication of stubborn sinfulness as much as an indication, born of our experience, that the conventional interpretation misses the point.

The most memorable line in the story is the oft decried admonition to "Eat, drink, and be merry," for tomorrow you may die. The underlying assumption among believers is that there is something wrong — cynical, if not sinful — about eating, drinking, and being merry in the face of death's certainty.

Such a conclusion flies in the face of the religious tradition out of which Jesus came, however. His spirituality was one which emphasized celebration and feasting. Clearly Jesus enjoyed a good party. While attending the wedding reception at Cana, he saw to it that there was plenty of good wine for everyone — 180 gallons by John's count! That must have been some party!

Later, he was carried away when feeding the multitudes by the sea and, after everyone had eaten their fill, there was enough food left over to fill 12 baskets with doggie bags.

Many of Jesus' parables about the kingdom of God draw on his own experience at dinner parties for their point. And let it never be forgotten that his critics found sufficient justification in his lifestyle to accuse him of being a "glutton and a drunkard (Luke 7:34)." Jesus was clearly a person who enjoyed eating, drinking and being merry.

The story, therefore, deserves another look.

On closer examination we discover that Jesus did not condemn the man for eating, drinking and being merry, nor even for being rich. Rather the man was called foolish for building bigger barns. The point of the story is that the entrepreneur was planning to store more of his wealth than he needed to eat, drink and be merry. Look again at the words of the story. The man says, "What shall I do for I have nowhere to store my crops?" Not true! He has barns. His problem is that his harvest has been so great that his present storage facilities will not hold all of the grain. So he decides, "I will tear down my barns and build larger ones, and there I will store all my grain. Then and only then will I have ample goods to eat, drink and be merry." Again, not true! He already has ample goods. He does not have to live in the moment. He has barns for his future. They may not be as big as he would like, but he has plenty to eat, drink and be merry. The man already has enough wealth to enjoy Shalom. He has a sense of well-being and security because God has generously blessed his land with fruitfulness. Fortune has smiled on him and he has been able to accumulate a sizeable portion of this world's goods.

The point of the story is not that there is something wrong with amassing some wealth, but that he was intending to store it all by building bigger barns and storing it would be lost. He was called "foolish" because he did not recognize that his wealth had brought him happiness and that it could do the same for others if only it were not locked up in those bigger barns. His sin was not that he had become wealthy, but that he wanted to hoard all his wealth. His sin was not that he ate, drank and was merry, but that he was withholding the means for others to do the same. He had become a bottleneck in the flow of Shalom blessings to others.

The story, so understood, is not a teaching condemning the foolishness of gathering wealth. It is rather a parable which condemns the refusal to share the wealth we do not need. It warns about the shortsightedness of failing to be a good custodian of the abundance that God entrusts to us.

Now that is a story with relevance for us as western Christians and one which we need to hear. You and I are, by any world measure of wealth, affluent people. I may not have great wealth, but measured by this world's standards, I have much wealth and it brings me and my family Shalom. It enables me

35

to eat, drink and be merry most of the time. It certainly conveys a sense of well-being that poverty doesn't. Nothing brings Shalom like a roof over your head and three square meals a day. Yet, we can eat only so much. Our closets can hold only so many clothes. We can live in only one place at a time. It is possible to draw the line at some point and say, "We have enough."

Nevertheless, our society has moved beyond the production of basic human needs to become a "consumer society" whose vitality and growth is maintained by convincing us that we need everything: a second car, an electric toothbrush, a new boat, a vacation home, a closet full of new clothes every time the fashions change. Government officials take great pride in pointing to an expanding economy, but it expands only by selling us goods and services that we do not need. We are a nation of bigger barn builders. We comprise only six percent of the world's population but consume forty percent of its goods. Collectively, we, too, are a bottleneck in the flow of Shalom to the rest of the world.

Jesus' parable, therefore, does have relevance. It raises the question, "How am I to regard my wealth, and what am I to do with it?" Sensitized to the plight of the world's oppressed peoples who are my brothers and sisters in Christ, I must now make a choice. I can either feel guilty about being wealthy and dispose of my goods as a danger to my spiritual health, or I can regard my wealth as a blessing showered for me for no more reason than the rain that falls on the just and the unjust; yet nevertheless to be used in the service of the Holy One.

To see my possessions as blessings from God is to realize that I have them on loan. I do not own them. A blessing is not something I earn, something for which I can take credit as if it was part of the cause and effect scheme of things. We have no ultimate claim on our blessings; otherwise they lose their blessed-ness. That I have them at all is a gift of grace which defies rational explanation. Why some are blessed with health and happiness, not to mention wealth, and others are not is a question which both puzzled and bothered the psalmists of old. It is an eternal mystery and a contemporary quandry. But that they have been entrusted to me is a fact I cannot escape. That they be put at God's disposal, therefore, is required. The Bible lays before us a radical concept of stewardship because it claims any hungry person has as much right to the bread in my freezer as I do; the shirt hanging unused in my closet belongs to anyone who needs it. The money that I plan to bank must be held in joint ownership with the poor. To say that my wealth is a blessing that brings Shalom, is to say in the strongest possible way: everybody and anybody in need has as much claim to it as I do. I do wrong to everyone I could assist but fail to help.

Our role as custodians to whom much has been given and of whom much is required is clarified if we make three affirmations about the much.

1. The much is from God. Wealth, as we have said, is a blessing from God and can bring Shalom into our lives. It is not sinful.

2. The much is sacramental. Wealth as a blessing is to be seen as a sacramental sign of God's love and trustworthiness. Its significance lies in directing our attention beyond itself to the Giver who stands behind the gift.

Annie Dillard tells a childhood story of occasionally hiding a precious penny of her own for someone to find, just for the excitement of it.[3] She recounts how she would draw big arrows on the sidewalk leading to it and label them, "Money ahead," or "This way to a surprise." Then she would watch from her hiding place, waiting for somebody — regardless of merit — to find her free gift of grace. She observes that the world is fairly strewn with lucky pennies flung broadside by some generous hand in the universe.

What a grace-full way to regard pennies and dollars! Lucky pennies are sacramental reminders of God's smiling presence. As sacramental signs, our dollars do not point to themselves as something to be held tightly, but rather beyond themselves to the trustworthy God who has strewn them in our path and hides in the shadows enjoying the Shalom they bring us. To confuse the sacramental sign with the thing signified is what the Bible means by idolatry. Hence, to clutch our dollars as if they were ends in themselves rather than seeing the hand that has cast them broadside in our pathway, is to become an idolater. Therein lies the danger of wealth about which the Bible is so concerned. But the danger does not diminish the sacramental function of wealth which is to remind us of the One who hides along our pathway. When we understand money sacramentally we can see that we are directed by our very wealth to trust in the God who feeds the birds of the air and provides fantastic fashions for the flowers of the field. God's provideence is secure; currency is not. It can be devalued, lost or stolen.

3. The much is to be shared. Wealth brings Shalom into our lives and, consequently, is to be shared with others because it has the power to bring Shalom into their lives as well. The right to private property is not an absolute. From a biblical perspective there is no such thing as private property because, as the Psalmist says, "The earth is the Lord's and the fullness thereof (Psalm 24:1)." The world's treasures, therefore, are God's and we are merely stewards of them for a time.

Returning then to the parable of the prosperous farmer who had to make a decision about building bigger barns to hold his surplus harvest, the story would have a different ending if the man had recognized he had enough and shared his surplus with others. He might even have been spoken of by Jesus as "rich toward God." But as it stands, the story addresses us as affluent western Christians.

Let us hype the point of it by supposing that we are millionaries. Now that is a consummation devoutly to be wished, but probably not a present prospect. Nevertheless, it is a fantasy worth entertaining for a moment.

If you had a million dollars what would you do with it? Specifically, how would you change the world? I find that an intriguing question. It is, in fact, the question of Shalom stewardship because a million dollars is more money than most of us need to eat, drink and be merry. The fact that we are now able to live on our present incomes would seem to suggest that we do not need much more. Some, perhaps, but for the most part we have enough. We are able to make do; able to eat, drink and be merry. Everything between our present income and a million dollars is surplus wealth. Consequently, if our dream came true and we inherited a million dollars from a rich uncle, we would suddenly find ourselves standing in the shoes of the rich man about whom Jesus was speaking. We would have more than ample goods and, like him, would be faced with the question of what to do with them. What are we to do with our over-abundance? Do we build bigger barns to store our wealth even though we do not need it? Or do we try to change the world a little because we believe in the power of wealth? Do we share the surplus with others — thereby, enabling them to eat, drink and be merry — or do we put it in the bank?

What about a half a million dollars? Or even a quarter of a million? Would there be any surplus money after expenses for eating, drinking and making merry?

Of course your present income may not be adequate for your present or anticipated financial needs. You may have children to put through not only college, but graduate school. Or aging parents to care for. But at some theoretical point on a monetary continuum it is possible to draw a line and say, "Enough! I can live with this amount and meet my responsibilities and fulfill my financial obligations." Everything beyond that figure, whether it be a million dollars, a half million, a hundred thousand, or a mere fifty thousand, everything beyond that point is surplus and can be given away without jeopardizing your own Shalom.

The relevant points for us to glean from Luke's story, therefore, seem to be at least the following:

1 — Like the rich farmer, who had much, all that we have is to be received gratefully as a blessing from God.

2 — Nevertheless, there is some level of wealth which is ample for us to eat, drink and be merry, just as there was for him.

3 — Unlike the rich man, however, we understand ourselves as stewards entrusted with our wealth for a time. We

are not merely to store it away but to put it to good use by sharing our surplus with others in direct proportion to the abundance of our blessing, as the Spirit of God indicates.

Jesus' parable invites us to boldly examine our financial resources and declare at what level we have enough. We do not have to squirrel more and more of our wealth away in bigger and better barns or savings accounts. There is some level at which each of us can say after cold sober reflection, "I have ample goods. Thank you, God!" Beyond that level Jesus invites us to consider sharing everything else with others. In the last analysis the measure of our faith is not how loudly we sing in church or how well we know the Bible. The measure of our trust in God is how tightly we grasp our billfolds.

Proper 14
Pentecost 12
Ordinary Time 19
Luke 12:32-40 [C, L]
Luke 12:32-48 [RC]

The Wisdom In Waiting

"Fear not!" Jesus says. These are the same words spoken by the angles to the Bethlehem shepherds on the occasion of his first coming. Now they are used to speak of his second coming. The reason why we need not fear is because God's good pleasure is to give us the kingdom. We cannot earn it. We cannot build it. It is a gift of grace. Despite all the evidence to the contrary and all attempts to oppose it, the promise has been made. The kingdom of God is on the way. We are to wait for it and be ready.

The second coming has fascinated believers from the beginning, wondering when, where, how it will take place. Speculations and predictions abound. Over-anxious believers have worked out all manner of time tables — all of them wrong, of course — but nevertheless purporting to read the signs of the times, fixing the seasons and marking the calendars. A lot of time, energy and anxiety could be saved by simply remembering Jesus' words on the matter, "No one knows, not even the angels . . . nor the Son, but the Father only (Matthew 24:36)." That's the bottom line. Further comment on the time, place and manner of the second coming is pointless. It is not for us to know. So we must wait.

Waiting for the kingdom to come is one of the disciplines of Christian faith. We pray for it every Sunday in the Lord's Prayer, but waiting is not easy. Most of us regard waiting as a necessary evil. The fact that sometimes it is necessary does not diminish our regard for it as an evil, or at least, undesirable. To wait in a long checkout line at the grocery store is irritating. To be stopped on the way home by a changing traffic light and then forced to wait until it turns green is annoying. To wait for a plane that is late in arriving is a waste of time.

Most of us are accustomed to filling our time with activities. We set schedules and measure ourselves against them so that we can know how much progress is being made. We make lists of things to be done and check off the items as each is accomplished. Indeed, our identity or sense of worth is tied up with our accomplishments. Waiting is consciously or unconsciously felt to be a threat to our self esteem. We have no patience with apparent lack of progress in ourselves or our society. Not to feel that day by day in every way we are becoming better and better is a vexing, if not depressing, realization.

The Apostle Paul even frets about the entire universe having to wait, groaning in travail, until its deliverance (Romans 8:22, 23). But he adds, "I consider that the sufferings of this present time are not worth comparing with the glory that is to be revealed to us. For the creation waits with eager longing for the revealing of the sons of God (Romans 8:18, 19)."

Even the Most High has to wait. We may wonder why Jesus was not sent a hundred years sooner. Why so long a wait? What was so special about that time? Those days? The gospel writers leave the speculations to our imagination. They simply say God had to wait for the "fulness of time (e.g., Mark 1:15 and Ephesians 1:10)." Even then, the Most High had to wait on the pregnancy of Mary. Nine long months had to be endured before God could bring the Word into the world.

Imagine the divine impatience as the little boy, Jesus, grew up one day at a time, maturing slowly into adulthood! First he had to learn to toddle and talk. The Word was burning to be spoken, but God had to wait. What an eternity that must have seemed for the Most High as the years slowly rolled by; waiting for Jesus to learn to talk, waiting while he gained the needed experience to speak the mature Word. Thirty more years the God of the Ages had to wait before the message was spoken. Those 30 years must have seemed as long to God as the preceding thirty centuries.

It would seem that waiting is a normal part of life. It takes time to heal physical and emotional injuries. A pregnancy cannot be hurried. Not even by God. It takes nine months, and all the impatience in the world or in heaven will not hurry the process along. It is a frustrated farmer who attends his scattered seed day and night hoping that by coaxing it along it will sprout and grow more rapidly. Not until the time is fulfilled will it do so. Waiting is his only option. We could observe that life does not reveal its meaning in a flash of insight. It unfolds over a period of time; year by year, experience after experience. There is no hurrying the process. We have to wait.

Jesus' words, however, are reassuring because they remind us that waiting is not only acceptable to God but intended by divine design. Rather than something to be regarded as a waste of time or a tolerated evil, waiting is a normative part of the life of faith. The kingdom comes to those who are willing to wait.

We may ask why is this so? What is the hidden wisdom in waiting?

Any attempt at an answer may be presumptuous, but at least two things appear to be true. First, we know from experience that when we are forced to wait it becomes abundantly clear we are not in control of the circumstances. Waiting is the vocation of the powerless. In our power conscious culture where being in charge is crucial to our identity and self esteem, waiting forces us to face the fact that someone else is running the show. It serves as a reminder, as indeed we occasionally need reminding, we are only human beings whose relation to God is characterized by not having, not seeing, not knowing and not grasping. Waiting delineates the boundary between our power and God's ability. Paul Tillich warns of the dangers in trying to ignore the boundary.

"A religion in which that is forgotten, no matter how ecstatic or active or reasonable, replaces God by its own creation of an image of God. Our religious life is characterized more by that kind of creation than anything else.

I think of the theologian who does not wait for God, because he possesses Him, enclosed within a doctrine. I think of the biblical student who does not wait for God, because he possesses Him, enclosed in a book. I think of the churchman who does not wait for God, because he possesses Him, enclosed in an institution. I think of the believer who does not wait for God, because he possesses Him, enclosed within his own experience."[4]

Waiting reminds us of our limitations and underscores the basic fact of human existence: we need God. The human equation is not complete without the divine factor. We are not the center of the universe nor is the Holy One at our beck and call. Being forced to wait emphasizes the fact that the power to deliver us from our bondage is not ours to command.

Paul's cry speaks for all of us, "I do not understand my own actions. For I do not do what I want, but I do the very thing I hate . . . I can will what is right, but I cannot do it. For I do not do the good I want, but the evil I do not want is what I do (Romans 7:15, 18, 19)."

When we have been overwhelmed by that kind of frustration we know that the power to change ourselves does not lie at our disposal. We can only long for the day of deliverance and the joy that cometh in the morning. Until then we have Christ's promise, "It is the Father's good pleasure to give you the kingdom."

That is why biblical Israel knew so much about waiting. In the opinion of the world, she was a third-rate power. In her saner moments she had no illusions about her ability to change the course of history nor hope of escaping her predicament as a pawn in the affairs of larger, more powerful nations. Israel knew that control of her destiny did not rest in her hands. Therefore, she looked forward to, and waited for, the coming salvation of the Lord.

By contrast, we can see why it is so difficult for us as Americans to wait. We suffer from a Messiah complex in which we assume that by our might we will bring peace and prosperity to the world. By flexing our military muscles we think we can enforce our will on others and with our technological prowess solve the problems of the world.

We carry this love affair with our capabilities right into our churches, where it is nourished by countless sermons the point of which seems to be that by flexing our motivational muscles and gritting our teeth, we can change ourselves and overcome our flaws. Perhaps we are disappointed with our slowness of heart. Filled with doubts, we find our faith a wooden thing, lifeless. Perhaps we are discouraged by our apparent lack of progress in overcoming some stubborn trait within ourselves which we can no longer tolerate. Or perhaps we are just plain tired of fighting some compulsion and feel that we are not winning the battle. We seem to take one step forward and two backward. Well-meaning religious cheerleaders urge us on from the side lines. "You can be a beautiful person, if you try. Work at it! Think positively!"

The problem with such assumptions is that the more sincere we are about doing something to make ourselves acceptable in our own eyes as well as God's, the more frustrating the struggle becomes.

Paul's arid frustration brought him to the oasis of God's grace. "Thanks be to God who gives us the victory (1 Corinthians 15:57)." That is, after all, the premise on which all of Jesus' talk about waiting is based. The good news is that the Holy One has the power to give us the kingdom even if we do not have the ability to create it within ourselves or our world. Waiting reminds us that we are not God and cannot push the stream. But it also reminds us that there is One who brings deliverance in the fullness of time.

This opens to us the other dimension in waiting's wisdom. The fullness of time always lies in the future. To wait, therefore, is to affirm that this present situation, this present condition, no matter how good or bad, is not the kingdom of God. Waiting presupposes that something is yet to happen, that the present is not the end of the adventure, that there is something yet to be hoped for and lived toward. The Old Testament reveals a long history of expectation making it clear that the

Christ was awaited a long time before his advent. And when he finally arrived he tells us we must be prepared to wait another long time for his coming again.

Waiting directs our attention to the future wherein our hope resides. The storytellers of the Bible almost always include a future tense when speaking of the saving power of God. Old Testament prophets refer to the coming day of the Lord when God will redeem the people. New Testament writers saw that day having arrived in Jesus' birth and life, but even when they spoke of it, they always included a future tense and spoke of his second coming. "It's not over," as the uncultured opera lover declared, "until the fat lady sings." Or in this instance, it's not over until the trumpets sound. Waiting invites us to live on tiptoes because the best view of the scene lies just over the horizon. To wait is to affirm that life is not all it can and will be. Not only is more to come, but the best is yet to be.

People who are content with the status quo have no future. It is the future which promises what is not yet, but which is looked toward with hope for its becoming. People who change society and make a difference in the way things are, are people who can wait. They live in the present, but have their eyes glued to the horizon. They live as though the future is where the fulfillment of their waiting is to be found. Their minds do not wander. Their attention does not stray. And they do not become cynical. Their hopes are fixed on the future and they wait, single-mindedly and expectantly, for the kingdom of God to come with its new creation. Nothing less will satisfy or fulfill them.

Visionaries who cannot wait are little more than social gadflies who come and go with the changing fashions and the latest fads. Which may be another reason why the Bible is so concerned about cultivating the ability to wait. The activists of the 60s crowded college campuses across the country. They were occupied with dreams of changing the world, creating a new society, righting the wrongs of the disenfranchised and redressing the grievances of the poor. But the world has gone about its entrenched ways for a long time and society proved to be a stubborn resistor to change. Neither yielded readily to their insistence. The wrongs were not redressed, the grievances were not corrected. As a result many of the student activists of the 60s at first became impatient, then cynical, and finally self-centered as they returned to their campuses to throw frisbees, looked inward through meditation, and graduated intent on making money. They could not wait.

Biblical faith, on the other hand, has sustained a social revolution for nearly 2,000 years because it has cultivated patience: the ability to wait. "The way to break down a brick wall," counseled a social reformer, "is not to attack it with a crowbar, but to lean on it until it gives way." The Old Testament prophet, Habakkuk, speaks of this patient pressure in a time of despair among his own people.

> *"For still the vision awaits its time;*
> *it hastens to the end — it will not lie.*
> *If it seems slow, wait for it;*
> *it will surely come, it will not delay."*
> *(Habakkuk 2:3)*

Israel's hope as a nation fed on such expectations. Her constituents literally bet their lives on them. Waiting for the fulfillment of the divine promise is as appropriate for our day as it was for Habakkuk's.

Waiting for the return of Christ is disciplined believing. It is living as though God is at work in our world even though we may not be aware of it or see any immediate evidence to support the claim. Precisely when all of the evidence seems to point to the contrary and there is no reason on earth to assume that we will ever be any different, or our world changed — when it seems we are plagued by the same old temper and jealousies, troubled by the familiar feelings of inadequacy and inferiority, living in a world of obstinate greed and injustice — precisely at that point we are to trust the promise made by the God of Abraham, Isaac and Jacob, not to mention Sarah, Rebekah and Rachel, and the God of our Lord Jesus Christ.

47

It is God's good pleasure to give us the kingdom. And because it is God for whom we wait, we can dance in the meanwhile and live as though it is on the way. The faithful Giver has promised a gift that carries a lifetime warranty, good forever.

Waiting for the kingdom, then, is an activity of faith. It is a skill to be valued and cultivated by every believer. It is not passive acquiescence nor is it born of futilty. Rather, it offers rehearsal time for practicing our relationship with God, affirming with the Psalmist of old that,

> *"I believe that I shall see the goodness of the Lord*
> *in the land of the living!*
> *Wait for the Lord;*
> *be strong, and let your heart take courage;*
> *yea, wait for the Lord (Psalm 27:13, 14)."*

A Faith That Burns

"Conflict" is a dirty word in most churches. As Christians, we seek to avoid it at all costs and do so in the name of Christian love. We call it, "seeking the peace, unity and purity" of the church.

And then Jesus comes along and says, "I have not come to bring peace, but a sword (Matthew 10:34)," or as Luke has it, "I came to cast fire upon the earth; and would that it were already kindled!" The words send us scurrying for explanations to reduce their caustic effect.

But who is this whose words intrude into our quiet worship, disturbing our Sabbath rest?

It is Jesus the outlaw! A law breaker! A radical and a revolutionary!

If we take off the rose colored glasses of traditional piety, Jesus stands before us in the gospel narratives as one who, when someone needed to be healed, ignored the Sabbath law banning work, and healed the person. Much to the dismay of the Pharisees, it might be added, those righteous representatives of the moral majority. He blatantly excused the breaking of the Sabbath law again when his freewheeling disciples plucked a few grains of wheat and ate them. The defense offered to the watching Pharisees was not that the disciples were starving to death — an argument which might have pardoned the offense — nor even that they were hungry, a more problematic defense. The law was bypassed, said Jesus, because the Sabbath was made for human beings not the other way around. Laws are relative; which is to say: Their authority is not absolute. They only exist to serve the interests of humanity and must be bypassed if they get in the way.

49

As a cute little baby, blowing bubbles and nursing at his mother's breast, Jesus made no enemies. But he outgrew his cradle. It was an adult Jesus, who taking responsibility for his actions and his words, fell off the popularity charts. His adoring public responded by demanding his execution. He was seen as a dangerous threat to the social order, a reckless blasphemer of God, and a corrupter of public morals. It is this Jesus who says, "I came to cast fire upon the earth; and would that it were already kindled!"

Jesus didn't get into trouble talking about the birds of the air and the lilies of the field. Indeed, healing the sick and blessing the children touched a warm and responsive cord in the crowds surrounding his ministry. Throngs were attracted by his charisma of love and compassion. But almost as if to correct a growing false impression, Jesus uttered these harsh words, "Do you think that I have come to give peace on earth? No, I tell you, but rather division; for henceforth in one house there will be five divided, three against two; and two against three; father against son, and son against father, mother against daughter and daughter against mother, mother-in-law against her daughter-in-law and daughter-in-law against her mother-in-law." Matthew even goes so far as to add, ". . . and a man's foes will be those of his own household . . . (Matthew 10:36)."

In light of his obvious concern and compassion we must wonder where Matthew and Luke dug up this quotation. The question has, in fact, led some scholars to conclude that these alien words were put in Jesus' mouth by the gospel writers in order to address the divisions emerging in the early church. But the sword of division about which Jesus spoke is the inevitable consequence of Christ-like love and there is no reason to doubt the authenticity of the teaching.

To love people as Jesus did is to stand for something. To stand for justice is to stand against injustice. To stand for truth is to oppose hypocrisy and falsehood. G. K. Chesterton observed that tolerance is the easy virtue of people who do not believe anything. Some unknown bard has put the observation poetically.

50

Popularity was his middle name.
Its prod was pride, its price was pain.
He never learned the word called, "no."
They spoke of him as "good old Joe."
His life was one long laughing spell,
*   and how he felt you couldn't tell.*
His favorite words were "yes," and "sure."
Yes, good old Joe was Simon Pure.
So when he died they wrote these lines,
*   and laid him down midst whispering pines.*
"Here lies a man — his name was Joe.
But what he stood for, we'll never know."

You couldn't have said that about Jesus. You knew where he was coming from. Clearly, "conflict," was not a dirty word in Christ's vocabulary. Yet, one of the more popular fantasies nurtured by a pietistic spirituality is that if folks could only be more loving, the world would be a better place. Peace and harmony would break out. What's more, if we would be more loving everyone would like us. Being a follower of Christ translates into being a nice man or woman. Not only will love iron out the differences between friends and enemies, but indeed, we ought not have any enemies. So the pop theology croons, "What the world needs now is love, sweet love!"

But in Jesus' view of things, love apparently does not mean that we refrain from conflict nor bow to the opposition. Jesus reminded his disciples that if everyone spoke well of them, something was wrong. We cannot pretend as though conflict does not exist. To be a Christian is to love all that Christ loved, and to be an enemy of all that crucified him. To follow him is to make enemies. Jesus did not win a popularity contest. He was awarded a cross and he bids us take up one and follow him.

"If the world hates you," Jesus warned, "know that it has hated me before it hated you. If you were of the world, the world would love its own; but because you are not of the world, therefore, the world hates you. Remember the word that I said to you, 'A servant is not greater than his master.' If they persecuted me, they will persecute you (John 15:18-20)."

Basic to all of Jesus' teaching was the assertion that all of us have worth in God's eyes; more worth than the lilies of the field, or the birds of the air. The poor, the meek, those who mourn; all are to be blessed. Those who are the outcasts of society, the lepers, the insane, the foreigners, those who have been ignored by the mainstream of life are the ones who have worth in God's sight. Jesus came to love in the name of the Holy One and that love has set a sword in our midst.

Jesus, himself, delineates the scope of that love. To love God, he says, is to love our neighbor; who, it must be noted, is not the person living next door but any needy person in the world. That covers a lot of uncomfortable ground. But the New Testament writers are adamant. If we cannot love our neighbor, whom we have seen, we cannot love God, whom we have not seen. The logic is devastating. John pulls no punches when he says that anyone who claims to love God while hating his brother is a liar (1 John 4:20). Not uninformed, not short-sighted, not ignorant. A bald-faced liar! In most circles, "them's fightin' words."

So, tell me! How do we say to the Bethlehem babe, "Well, concern for the poverty plagued shepherds is a matter of opinion?" How can I say to Emmanuel — God with us, born in a barn and crucified on a cross — that my child's education is more important than that of the kid in the ghetto?

Or, how do you say to the Christ who had nowhere to lay his head that it is more important for you to live in a $100,000 house than it is to provide public housing, and therefore, you will vote against a tax increase because its passage would mean cutting back on your vacation this year. In a world where we, who must diet to reduce our overweight while three-quarters of its population goes to bed hungry at night — how do we say to the Bread of Life, "I can't afford to tithe?"

To take on the name of Christ as a "Christian" is to be radically bonded to those who have been overlooked by the distributors of this world's goods and services; those who were born, or must live in the "barns" of this world. For us who assume that Jesus is the Christ reaching out to those who have to scrape the bottom of the barrel is the ethical imperative. This means doing what Jesus did by becoming involved in the lives of those who are regarded as less than beautiful by the usual standards of society: economic, social and moral. That point seems dangerously close to being missed by many of us as Christians in this country. Today, multitudes of our people look upon their spiritual journeys as a religious quest in search of personal fulfillment. The rise of the huge array of nondenominational parachurch organizations and Bible study movements that have captured the allegiance of millions, offers a personalized perspective of the Gospel story which panders to this market. The emergence in the late 1960s of the Charismatic Renewal Movement has further emphasized a personal, individualized faith. The religious landscape has been enlarged to include a rapidly growing number of churches that do not identify themselves with any of the historic denominations. All are aggressively seeking converts. Because of thinning numbers in mainline churches and the need for supporters in the newer religious groups, the drive toward self preservation is in the end stronger than the desire for social change. Whether because of fear, or tiredness, or boredom, or change in the national temperament, the causes of the 60s have given way to different priorities in the 80s and 90s. Virtually every public opinion poll comes up with essentially the same results: the concern for social justice and human rights is losing ground in the search for an individualized spirituality and numerical growth.

But numerical growth is our concern. To love as Christ loved, is God's. Jesus' words are a constant reminder to us that the name of the game is setting fire to the old so that the new can emerge. The old wineskins cannot hold the new wine of the Spirit. "Do not think that I have come to bring peace!" The good news of God's love is often bad news for people of privilege and power, because in Jesus, God provides a higher authority than the law of the land or religious practice. The Word enfleshed in Jesus gives all oppressed people permission to live as free men and women. When Jesus says, "Peace,

peace, I leave with you. My peace I give to you, but not as the world gives (John 14:27)," he is not talking to tired, hassled executives who deserve a little rest. On the contrary, he is offering himself as that higher authority to those who labor under the burden of social sin; those who are milked by it, drained by it, used by it. Jesus is telling them that he has come to give them the Shalom that the world will not give. Set within the biblical purview of God's concerns, this is a revolutionary invitation to those victimized by society. It is divine permission to lay hold of that Shalom which society denies them. It is an open invitation to take it if the world will not share it.

Jesus represents a long biblical tradition of what, from the perspective of Pilate and Pharaoh, champions of the status quo, must have been considered left wing political and economic views. The Exodus was a political revolution, though that reality may have escaped our notice in the Sunday school version of the tale. It involved the tactics of intimidation and force. Its results were violence and bloodshed. What is disturbingly clear in the biblical account is: not only is God praised by the Hebrew slaves for their deliverance from bondage, but the Holy One is credited with having masterminded the whole plot, including the bloodshed.

Our instinctive inclination is to dismiss such a dreadful bias in the story by claiming, for ourselves, a less bloodthirsty understanding of God; one which pictures God taking little lambs into the Divine bosom and gently leading those who are with young. We, thereby, turn the Lion of Judah into a household pet, tamed and domesticated. Jesus as the messianic King is emasculated as a court eunuch and becomes the private chaplain to tired corporate executives who are exhausted from their efforts to increase profits. "Come to me, all you who labor and are heavy laden, and I will give you rest. Peace, I leave with you." We have sentimentalized God's love, just as we have so many of the stories surrounding the King.

The birth narratives of Jesus, and the seasonal sentimentality surrounding them, are a case in point. They were never written as Christmas stories to be acted out in Sunday school pageants by people wearing bathrobes. We have trivialized these gospel stories, not to mention those of his life, death and Resurrection. As a result Christmas and Easter have become cultural rituals; times for families to gather, go to church, and celebrate traditions. They have become holidays in our society featuring Santa Claus and Easter bunnies, and offering opportunity for economic gain. But they are almost devoid of any serious reflection about their theological, much less political significance.

Herod, however, did not miss the point! The coming of Christ was a political event with revolutionary implications, and Herod knew it. Matthew's narrative includes the cruel slaying of innocent children (Matthew 2:13-18). And why? Because the power of Herod was threatened. He sensed in this Divine visitation something that would challenge Caesar's law and order, alter the priorities of his people and render relative his authority. Herod was so threatened and enraged that he began a systematic liquidation of all the male children two years of age and under. He was taking no chances.

Today we are surprised by the abrasive words of Jesus reported by Luke, but Luke might well have said, "What did you expect? Chimes?" Luke telegraphs his punch by recording, at the beginning of his Gospel, the psychic foresight of Mary, the mother of Jesus, regarding the ominous implications of her son's Messianic reign.

> *"He has shown strength with his arm,*
> *he has scattered the proud in the imagination of their*
> *hearts,*
> *he has put down the mighty from their thrones,*
> *and exalted those of low degree;*
> *he has filled the hungry with good things,*
> *and the rich he has sent empty away."*
> *(Luke 1:51-53)*

That is cause for concern if you happen to be rich, full or mighty. Compared to the standards by which most of the world's population lives, all of us probably fall into one or more of these categories. As I read Mary's prophecy, that causes me a fair amount of anxiety. Her perspective is of those victimized by the privileged brokers of worldly power.

Jesus' words have lit a fire in our midst and something is apt to be incinerated. He was, after all, a subversive and the telling of his story has revolutionary implications for us. We must never forget that the church's scriptural source of wisdom, without hesitation or apology, asserts that a nation which fuels its economy on greed, that is, at the expense of others' basic needs, is not only a nation under God; it is a nation under God's judgment. The sword of divine justice hangs over us. Amidst all of the sloganeering and flag waving it must seriously be questioned by us as Americans — and especially those of us who salute the Christian flag — if we are genuinely concerned about meeting the needs of those for whom Christ gave the last full measure of devotion?

Two Doors; One Choice

In *The Lady And The Tiger*, Frank Stockton sets before the reader the dilemma of a gladiator who faces his fate in the arena standing before two doors. He must choose which of them to open. Behind one door waits a hungry tiger. Behind the other, a lovely maiden.

Jesus presents us with a similar dilemma in this parable. Behind one door to the kingdom waits the tiger of divine wrath. Behind the other door stands the fair maiden of grace. The parable is offered in response to the worried question, near to the heart of every believer, "Is it true, that only a few will be saved?" Jesus admits that many want to enter the kingdom and be saved. He envisions a crowd, clamoring at the entrance to get in. But the door will be closed and locked to them. Grace will not be granted to the multitudes battering the gates of heaven. Nevertheless, Jesus offers a hint for those who want to avoid the rush. What is not available to the masses of seeking pilgrims can be obtained, one person at a time, if they will strive to enter by way of the narrow door. Though many are seeking salvation, the door that seems so obviously the entrance to the kingdom of God is closed and locked. Its appearance is deceiving. Its promise of salvation is false.

But what is this counterfeit way to the throne of grace sought by so many? And what does it mean to enter through the narrow door?

Many believers think the Christian faith can be summed up in the "golden rule." Do unto others what you would have them do unto you. Christians have interpreted the narrow door to be that of living a good life. For some it means living by the creed, "I don't smoke and I don't chew, and I don't go

57

with girls that do!'' Thus Jesus is heard to say, "Strive to behave yourselves. Deny yourself, take up your cross and follow me through the narrow door into the kingdom of God.'' The crowd, it is assumed, are the sinners who have been indulging themselves with this world's pleasures, and who at the last minute, try to barge in at the main entrance only to find it closed in judgment. Those, on the other hand, who have bit the bullet of disciplined obedience are able to slip safely through the side door. Sound familiar?

The problem with this interpretation is that it ignores the fact that everyone in the parable is sincerely seeking entrance to the kingdom. Those who get in are no less sinful than those left on the steps. Indeed, those at the front door can boast impressive religious pedigrees. They are the sons and daughters of Abraham. No doubt their credentials include letters of moral recommendation. The difference is not in the taint of their lives but in their choice of doors.

The great masses of those concerned with heavenly issues believe that human nature is prone to sin and disobedience, which in turn, requires large doses of contrition and confession to counteract the condition and allow penitent believers to pass customs at the borders of the kingdom. Righteousness and repentance are what pleases God. Righteousness means living a morally superior life while repentance means being sorry for our sinful nature and bending our evil wills away from their natural inclinations in order to make them conform to God's will. Obedience to the divine will is seen as the narrow doorway that leads to heaven and it swings on the rusty hinges of "shoulds" and "oughts." "You should do this" "You ought not to do that."

Alas, this approach is also the way of pharisaical religion and doesn't allow for much flexibility, forgiveness or fun. Garrison Keillor speaks of puritans as those believers who suspect that somewhere out there people are enjoying themselves. But fun aside! Pharisaical religion is characterized by self-righteousness; the sure knowledge of the difference between right and wrong, good and bad, truth and heresy, those inside the circle of grace and those on the outside. Righteous living — that is, obedience to the law — was the major concern of pharisaical religion at the time of Jesus, and it is significant that he was at such odds with them over it.

A religion of requirements demands a piety of self-denial to be obedient to God's greater will. "What would Jesus do?" is a popularized way of putting the ethical question. Never mind that we have no idea what Jesus would do in the complex inter-relationships of today's technological society. Never mind that the question is simplistic. The problem with the attempt to be like Jesus is that it does away with our individuality. The fact of the matter is, Jesus never required his disciples to become like him. He loved and honored their uniqueness. He cherished their diversity. He did not try to iron out their idiosyncrasies; he saw them as gifts.

Peter, for example, had a spitfire temper and the impetuosity of a school boy. A psychiatrist would have said, "That's going to be a problem for a church leader. Better get some counseling or not enter the ministry." But Jesus looked at his neurosis and said, "That's the rock-like quality on which I can build a church (cf. Matthew 16:18)."

In 1933 Carl Jung observed in his book, *Modern Man In Search Of A Soul,* that it is no easy matter to live a life modeled on Christ, but it is unspeakably more difficult to live one's own life as truly as Christ lived his. The question for Christians living today is not, "What would Jesus do?" for he has not left us here to live his life as a clone, but to live our own. No one can do my living for me, or dying either, for that matter. God has not given my life to you, nor your life to someone else. No one but you will be held accountable for it.

It is written of Zusya — the old Rabbi of Annitol — that shortly before his death he gathered his disciples around him and said, "When I die and stand before my heavenly Judge, God will not say to me, 'Zusya, why weren't you Moses?' No! God will say to me, 'Zusya, you could at least have been Zusya . . . so why weren't you?' "

Jesus summarized the total of our obligations before God with just two requirements: Love God, and your neighbor as yourself. In the mad scramble of religious people to enter the kingdom, the self is often trampled by the crowd. In church circles we sometimes call this self-denial "humility," or worse, "obedience." Yet, only by loving ourselves and discovering the amazing miracle of our own being, can we love and be amazed at the miracle of another person's life. There are no two of us alike. Therefore, denying ourselves and becoming selfless is blasphemous to the Creator God who went to a lot of trouble creating an infinite variety of human beings, each with its own unique identity. What is needed, is not a reaffirmation of the self-denying piety which suffocates our individuality and leads nowhere, but a new piety of self-affirmation; a narrow door to Life through which we must come individually, one at a time.

Jesus offers us a glimpse of this narrow door which leads to the banquet table of God in the parable of the Prodigal Son (Luke 15:11-24). There, Jesus speaks of an adventurous lad who demanded his share of the family fortune and then squandered it with loose living in a "far country." The lost lad eventually "came to himself" and returned home where he was sumptuously fed by dad. Apparently, the reason the father handed over his son's share of the inheritance in the first place — knowing that he was headstrong and would most likely lose it — was because he knew there was no short cut to his son's finding himself. If he had insisted on the boy's staying at home and toeing the mark as the elder brother did, the lad would have remained undefiled but hopelessly lost. In the parable it is clear that defilement and sin are useless categories for understanding what Jesus means by salvation. To be saved is to discover who we are and feel at home with ourselves. We are saved when we come to ourselves, whether that be by staying at home or journeying to the far country. Such an understanding of salvation lifts our discussion out of the realm of moralist thinking and allows us room to grow in the fullness of our personhood.

The parable of the prodigal gives us another way of understanding the salvation wrought by Jesus. Rather than the One who forgives us when we are disobedient, Jesus tells a story of someone who came to himself and returned home, a little older and undoubtedly wiser. But notice! The young man does not return home with a faith focused on Christ's atoning sacrifice. The young man has, to be sure, composed and rehearsed a confession of shortcomings worthy of many printed prayers used in churches today. In fact, he tries to deliver his prepared statement in the presence of his father. But the father interrupts him. He has no interest in his son's confession of sin. Disobedience and defilement do not even enter the conversation. They are not issues so far as the father is concerned. Instead, he wants to party with the son who was lost and is found, dead and is now alive.

The view of the kingdom that Jesus gives us in this story is radically different from that held by the crowd: parents, teachers, employers, clergy. Their assumption is that we need to "shape up or ship out." The stories they tell us are based on conditional love. "If you obey me then I will love you and let you come into my house."

Jesus, by contrast, portrays God as a parent who accepts us as we are. Accepted, that is! Not simply forgiven. There is no reason to assume that just because the prodigal came home he lost his appetite for good food and fine wine, nor his appreciation for beautiful women. He was not forgiven. He was accepted for who he was, a lad who had to go into the far country to find himself.

For this kind of salvation, the wide door of living by righteous prescriptions will not do. We come home, not with the clamoring crowds trying to impress God with our credentials of goodness, but one person at a time, through the narrow door of self-discovery.

Carl Jung regards the second half of life as having unique significance for the individual's self understanding. He believes we spend the formative years taking our identity cues from the world around us. Significant others define our values, roles, and self-image. Our identities depend upon measuring up to the expectations of family, school, the work place, church and society. We want to take our place responsibly within their ranks.

But, claims Jung, the major task of the maturing individual is to get in touch with the inner self and especially that unconscious portion of the psyche that holds the key to our true identity. The person that we have consciously become is largely the product of the crowd's wishes and our reaction to them. The unconscious, however, is not concerned about the wishes of the world, nor the external authorities that prescribe beliefs and behavior for us. The unconscious only cares about the real self that has been lying dormant like a seed waiting for springtime. It is during this second half of life that the seedling of identity begins to sprout and push itself into consciousness.

It takes courage to affirm this identity because it frequently goes against the grain of public expectations and the crowd's convenience. To take responsibility for our lives and the choices by which we determine them is always risky and, therefore, frightening. Some are never able to do it. Unfortunately, churches are crowded with people desiring the kingdom but who do not know themselves. They are busy knocking at the wide door while it is the narrow door that holds the promise. They have stopped listening to their inner voice and listen only to the authority figures who tell them what to do, how they ought to behave, and what values they should be living by. What Jesus calls his followers to risk requires courage. It means entering through the narrow door alone!

In the legend of King Arthur and the knights of the Round Table, a vision of the holy grail comes to Sir Gawain. He vows to set off in search of it the very next day. All the other knights of the Round Table vow that they, too, will go in search of the sacred chalice. But they will not journey together. As dawn breaks the following morning, each of the knights enters the forest alone, where he perceives it to be the darkest and the thickest. None of the knights follow a pathway. To do so would be to go where someone else had already searched.

To find ourselves, like the search for the holy grail, is not something we can do by walking someone else's path. No one can show us the way. It is, rather, a search we carry on by ourselves. It is the internal search for the possibility of our own becoming. My high school band director was frequently greeted with silence when he gave the downbeat. No sound at all! As fledgling musicials, we were unsure of ourselves, each of us hesitating, waiting for someone else to risk the first note. In exasperation the director threw down his baton — like a gauntlet thrown down in challenge, I suppose — and demanded, "I'd rather have a good big loud mistake than no sound at all." His word of permission moved us to oblige him with multitudes of mistakes, but in between, there was some recognizable music. In the case of our band, it seemed to be a case of not being able to have the one without the other.

So with life. Of course, mistakes will be made by such daring. Of course, others may be hurt. Of course, some things will be left undone. Of course, some sins will be committed. But there is no alternative if we are to live.

Lowell Streiker portrays both the agony and ecstasy of our dilemma.

"Maturity or self-realization requires that I become aware of the unique, irreplaceable potentialities of my existence as a person and that I accept the responsibility for actualizing them. Self-realization is a painful, gradual process marked by many reversals, defeats and disappointments. Since what I was meant to be is different from what anyone else was meant to be, no formula, maxim, generalization, or dogma can distinguish for me between the real and the apparently real. Life is exposure to contradiction, error, guilt and regret. Its deepest lessons are taught the worst of all possible ways. Man is the only creature with potential, but this potential is found only in, through, and despite the bumbling, awkwardness of human development. (We) become men and women by risking regret, accepting guilt, and learning from failure."[5]

63

They know, even if we do not, that sin is a fact of human existence, as is the color of our eyes or the set of our jaws. The only possible ethical imperative, therefore, is — as Luther would remind us — to sin to the glory of God. The alternative is to curl up in some womb-like corner and choose not to risk living at all.

To be saved means that each of us, in our own way, can risk living, which in turn, means we can risk sinning. When we recognize that to live is to sin, we relax and sin to the glory of God. You might not say that to just anybody, but you would say it to those who are serious about entering the kingdom of God. For only as we are given permission to sin to the glory of God can we risk coming to ourselves through the narrow door and celebrating at the table of the Lord the miracle of our being.

Kingdom Etiquette

This parable of Jesus is often treated as a call for humility. When invited out for dinner, stand aside and let others be seated first. If that is its purpose it seems to be much ado about very little. But to interpret his words as a teaching on self effacement is to miss the point of the parable. Jesus told parables to describe the kingdom of God not to give lessons in social etiquette. Here, Jesus apparently used the occasion of his sabbath's dinner invitation to tell yet another parable about the kingdom of God which he frequently likened to a feast. What moved him to speak this time was his observation of how the invited guests ungraciously sought the seats of honor, and then were asked to move to make room for those for whom the seats had been reserved. The point of the parable is that in the kingdom of God we come as shirt-tail relatives to the marriage feast of the Lord and discover to our amazement that the host has saved the places of honor for us. Rather than being last on the invited guest list, we are called "friends" of the groom in the presence of all. Our true identity, says Jesus, is not that of a distant acquaintance. We are among those who sit with the most High as Christ's friends and equals.

We may have difficulty thinking of ourselves in such familiar terms much less worthy of honor in the kingdom. We have been fed a heavy diet of self-effacement. Very early in the history of the church, a personal piety of self-denial came into vogue. Indeed, by the time Paul wrote his letter to the church at Rome he was already imploring his readers not to think of themselves more highly than they ought to think (Romans 12:3). Taking up our cross daily and following Jesus came to mean emptying ourselves of all personal pride, ambition and self-worth in order to do God's will which was loving and serving others. Love of neighbor was understood as antithetic to love of self and was to be done at the expense of personal ambition. Early Christian spirituality developed an individual ethic of self-sacrifice for the sake of others and religion has been influenced by it ever since.

Consequently, as believers, we have been admonished from infancy to be "servants of God." And if you missed that one, you could not have gone to church without being addressed as a "sinner." The label was reinforced by the message we got, and gave, at home. As parents, we loved our children and did our best for them with Spock in one hand and Scripture in the other. But any psychologist will tell you that we also probably passed on to them a negative self-image as we scolded and molded their behavior to fit into socially acceptable patterns. The first words that my children learned to say were, "No! No!" As a result of a lifetime of conditioning it is hard to believe new stories about ourselves.

But that is exactly what Jesus invites us to do when he hands us an invitation to the banquet of the kingdom. We are to come as his friends and sit with him as honored equals.

Later, as Jesus gathered with his disciples for their last supper together, he dramatically enacted his own parable. He told them, "No longer do I call you servants, for the servant does not know what his master is doing; but I have called you friends, for all that I have heard from my Father I have made known to you (John 15:15)." And then he added, "I tell you I shall not eat . . . again until it is fulfilled in the kingdom of God (Luke 22:16)." It was the last meal before the feast of the kingdom at which Jesus and his friends will gather.

There are probably few words in all of Scripture that are more explosive than these. They are all the more dangerous because they appear so innocent. Less than 24 hours after Jesus invited the disciples to be his friends, they were running scared. Not one of them wanted to be known as a friend of Jesus. It was too risky. Far better to live as a servant of the Master than to be a friend of the accused. There is, after all, a certain security in being a servant. A servant cannot be blamed for the actions of the Master. A servant simply reports for duty and carries out orders. Nor does a servant have to think or make decisions. A servant bears no responsibility and takes neither credit nor blame. It was a defense often heard at the Nuremberg trials, and more recently, one used by Oliver North in the Contragate affair.

Freidrich Nietzsche drew the distinction between a servant morality and a master morality with disturbing clarity. A servant morality adopts values and follows a morality which is imposed upon us by others. It negates the self. A master morality, on the other hand, sees the self as the creator of both values and morality. It, therefore, affirms the self. Nietzsche saw religion as the great espouser of servant morality because it portrayed values and morals as absolutes given by God. He contended that to be fully human is to realize that morality is something we create. Values are not hung "out there" like stars in the sky. We are the ones who do the valuing. The clues to ethical behavior come from within ourselves and are not prescribed for us by some external authority. Values are neither objective nor carved in stone despite the claims of the church. Instead, they come from an internal gyroscope that guides the course of our lives.

Those internal proddings are what the hymn writer, James Montgomery, must have had in mind when he spoke of "the soul's sincere desire." When we learn to listen to them we begin to trust them, for these stirrings of the soul speak with an urgency and wisdom that is experienced as divine will. They tell us what is crucial for our lives to be whole and good.

Mary Richards counsels,

> "We have to trust the invisible gauges we carry within us. We have to realize that a creative being lives within ourselves, whether we like it or not, and that we must get out of its way, for it will give us no peace until we do."[6]

Here, modern psychotherapy can help us. We begin by listening to ourselves at the deepest levels of our being: dreams, intuitive hunches, fantasies. As we come to understand the language of symbolism, decipher its meaning and trust its message, we find that, in fact, we are listening to God. We become aware that these communiques emerging from the depths of our being are the voice of Being itself speaking to us. They constitute what the Bible calls, "the still, small Voice." It was what the prophet Elijah heard (cf. 1 King 19). Not in the booming of earthquake, fire, or wind, all of which are symbols of the Divine presence and Spirit, but in the inner stirrings of intuition. Elijah only heard the Word of God when he was quiet enough to listen to the still, small voice within himself.

This is not to suggest that God cannot speak through the earthquake, fire and wind. Karl Barth once graphically reminded his students that God can speak through Russian Communism, a flute concerto or a dead dog. But the mystical tradition within the Christian faith has largely been forgotten or ignored by mainline churches. With the over-reaction of the Protestant Reformation to the hierarchial authority of the church, Protestant orthodoxy enthroned the Bible and preaching as the premier means by which God speaks to believers. As a result, the Protestant tradition has all but lost the discipline of listening to the still, small voice. When silence is included in worship as part of the liturgy, both God and the believer had better have on track shoes. The silence can be timed in milliseconds. Get ready! Get set! Go! Before we can settle into the silence, the next hymn is being announced or someone is nudging us to pass the offering plate. For the most part we feel uncomfortable with silence in our relationships with others, and certainly with God.

The Quakers, of course, are an exception, and have managed to continue practicing the discipline of silence. They include great quantities of it in their gatherings. They speak of this voice within as the "inner light," which provides the believer with internal illumination for seeing the direction in which God is pointing. The point to be grasped, however, is that this inner guidance is not derived from some blueprint drawn for us by others. It only comes by sensing and responding to those nudges from within.

It takes courage to heed these nudges for it means daring to affirm ourselves. To take responsibility for our lives as Jesus did is always risky and, therefore, frightening. We can understand the anxiety that overtook the Hebrew slaves after they escaped from their Egyptian masters. It produced an identity crisis. Forty years of maturing in the wilderness were required before they could accept their new identity. It meant taking responsibility for their freedom as God's people. After years of bondage they had a slave mentality and were used to taking orders. None of them had ever needed to think before or take responsibility for themselves. In the wilderness, condemned to God's freedom, they began to complain to Moses, "What have you done to us, bringing us out into the wilderness to die? Better if you had left us slaves of the Egyptians. At least, they took care of us. But out here in the wilderness, living as free people, trusting only God, that's too risky." It took four decades for them to believe the new story. Freedom and maturity demand a price. So does salvation. "Work it out," says Paul, "in fear and trembling."

Of course, we long for the security of the servant because it simplifies our relationship with God. We simply live by the law. Servants may obey or disobey the commands of their Master, but at least there is no confusion about what is required; and there is always the option of asking the Master's forgiveness when they fail. The great boon about which the church speaks is the Divine mercy made available to repentant sinner/servants. God makes everything right through the sacrifice of Jesus on the cross. The piety of a servant hinges on obedience or disobedience, and in disobedience the servant can always hope for forgiveness.

But the piety of the friend means we must accept the responsibility for our own life as Jesus accepted responsibility for his.

It takes courage to accept Jesus' invitation to the banquet. It means affirming ourselves as his equals. And the courage does not remove the guilt or despair. Courage, rather, must affirm the guilt and despair by taking them into our identity. As we have said, the piety of the servanthood offers the option of forgiveness when we fail and fall. But the piety of equality offers no such succor. To be spiritually mature means daring to accept Jesus as our Teacher and Friend, rather than our Lord and Master. It means taking full responsibility for our decisions and our actions, even as it did for him. Spiritual maturity means making choices before God and suffering the consequences before the world. The buck stops with us. Instead of forgiveness, we must accept the guilt and despair that go with the risk of trusting our own instincts and being wrong.

Discerning God's will requires developing a trust in the credibility and integrity of our own being. Very risky business indeed! There are no guarantees in advance that we will not be mistaken. We can submit our judgments to the community of faith for their support, critique, or modification, but in the last analysis we must stand alone before the throne of grace and give an accounting for our choices.

Our understanding of confession, therefore, is radically altered. We make confession of our sins, not in order to remove them and their surrounding guilt, but to affirm both courageously before God. We are invited to risk being ourselves. We must accept the responsibility for our lives and affirm, as a part of them, the guilt and despair that go with living. In this parable Jesus calls us to put a servant mentality behind us. No longer are we to think of ourselves as servants of our Lord and Master. We are encouraged to become his friends and take our place with him at the table of the Lord.

It boils down to a matter of identity. We either think of ourselves as the servants of the Lord with certain duties to perform, or we think of ourselves as his friends with certain privileges to enjoy.

The gospel, or good news, is that Christ reveals our true worth. We have value, sacred value. We are somebody because we sit with him in the places of honor at the kingdom banquet.

70

To realize this truth about ourselves is empowering in the face of the principalities and powers of this world. It can certainly threaten existing social structures, political and economic, and all of the prescribed roles that make their "systems" work. This discovery of self worth — grace, if you will — is dangerous to the life of any social institution because it renders relative their self-serving claims of importance. For example, the emergence of feminism in the church, with its insistence that women, no less than men, can wear the mantle of spiritual leadership, has jolted and jarred the patriarchal assumptions of ecclestiastical bureaucrats.

The results of empowerment can be seen in the restless awakening of third world peoples. They are tired of being nobodies; tired of being the servants of western capitalistic colonialism. The novelty has worn off. Many of the political leaders of these third world nations have been educated in missionary schools where they have heard this revolutionary Word. What is more, they have come to believe it. They are no longer content to be the world's second class citizens. They think of themselves as being sacred worth in the eyes of God.

During the dark days of slavery in this country, Blacks worked in the cotton fields stripped of their dignity, naked to the waist, and barefoot in the dirt. But the human spirit refuses to be broken. From deep within the Black psyche rose that rebellion spawned by Christian faith and expressed in the music of the soul; the Negro spirituals. In them the note of human dignity is never far from the praise of God.

I got shoes, you got shoes,
All of God's chillun got shoes.
When I get to heav'n, gonna put on my shoes.
I'm gonna walk all over God's heav'n.

What does it mean to sit in the seats of honor at the kingdom table? It means dropping a barefooted slave mentality! It means putting on our heavenly shoes, and walking all over God's heaven and God's good earth, as well. To be an honored guest at the feast of the Lord is to value oneself ultimately.

The etiquette of the kingdom requires us to accept Jesus' invitation to the marriage banquet. To do so carries with it a fair amount of anxiety because spiritual growth means trusting the voice within rather than those voices which have claimed our allegiance before. It also means risking the wrath of those deposed powers and principalities.

So, we stand at the door of the banquet hall alone and knock timidly. The door swings open. The red carpet has been laid, the tables are set, the other guests have all arrived. The Host smiles warmly and comes to greet us. He holds out his hand. "Friend!" he says, "Come up here and sit with me!"

Counting The Cost

"Come to me all of you who labor and are heavy laden and I will give you rest!" Christ's warm invitation to discipleship is appealing and difficult to resist. Understandably, the lines were long. Seekers crowded around him, aware that something was missing in their lives; sensing that this man of grace could fill the empty places.

The widespread interest of people in spiritual matters is the key to understanding the significance of his apparent rebuff in these verses. The warning to would-be disciples is given by Jesus to these great multitudes of religious groupies; spiritual camp followers, as it were. Discipleship is expensive. What cost Jesus his life, costs us ours. There is no such thing as "cheap grace." The temptation is always to soften his words, tame them, and make Jesus and his message more winsome. But let them stand as they are without attempting to make the rough places plain. After all, there are those more experienced in discipleship than we who have verified his words at the expense of their lives. Dietrich Bonhoeffer reminds us that when Christ calls us into discipleship he bids us come and die. There are, of course, many ways to die although Bonhoeffer paid for his discipleship with a martyr's death. But all would-be disciples must take on the mind of Christ and the burdens of love that he bore. Jesus asks, "Can you share your life with others? Can you extend your love beyond the boundaries of family loyalty? Can it transcend your commitment to life itself?" It is in this context that Jesus warns, "Calculate the cost, Sisters and Brothers, before signing on for a tour of duty."

Revivals of religious interest periodically sweep the country. Most recently an apparent spiritual re-awakening is moving

73

in the hearts of middle class Americans. A senior vice president of a major company, who found religion, summarizes the feelings of many converts. "Before, I wanted to be successful in the world; now I want to exalt the Lord. I want to stay a businessman, but I want people to know that God changes lives."

The tune has a familiar ring to it. The biblical story of Nicodemus comes forcefully to mind: Nicodemus, that middle-class, fairly well-to-do man of prestige and stature in the community. Yet with all of his comforts, he was vaguely uneasy about himself, sensing that something was lacking. He came to Jesus to talk religion.

As middle class Americans, we, like Nicodemus, feel a certain lostness and want a sense of certainty. And like Nicodemus, we hunger to know that God loves us, as we are, that God blesses us, as we are, and that God gives us permission to be as we are. "I want to stay a businessman, but I want people to know that God changes lives." Changes lives, yes! But not our values! Not society! Not our company. Our brother wants to stay with the system. He wants to remain a vice president in good standing with the company. Like Nicodemus, multitudes of us — comfortable, fairly well-to-do, enjoying some status in the community, well thought of by our peers — nonetheless come to Christ to talk about religion, hungry to know that God loves us as we are, blesses us as we are, and gives us permission to be as we are.

And why not? There's nothing wrong with the way we are. Americans, God fearing people, and proud of it. Humility demands that we admit we need a little fixing up here and there; some tinkering around the edges. But we are, after all, a nation under God. Leaders of the free world; champions of God, motherhood, and a sound dollar. The American way is the only way because it is God's way.

For most of us the kingdom of God and the American way are comfortable bed-fellows. The German sociologist, Max Weber, noted that Calvinism — because of its belief in human sinfulness, i.e. selfishness; coupled with its call to frugality —

fostered and nurtured a capitalistic economic system. Roman Catholic philosopher and theologian, Michael Novac, believes that capitalism works better than any other economic system because we are sinners. "I believe in sin," he said. "Socialism is a system built on belief in human goodness; so it never works. Capitalism is a system built on belief in human selfishness; given checks and balances, it is nearly always a smashing, scandalous success."[7] The two systems of thought fit together so well, in fact, that Capitalism has become a quasi-religion in our society. No one dares criticize it for fear of being called un-American. Politics and religion merge in the creedal statements, "I own what I have." "I earned it." "It is mine to do with as I please." "Let others get theirs the same way I did."

From a Christian perspective we must admit that the legacy of the Reagan years has legitimized selfishness. "Why do I owe my neighbor anything?" has become a respectable question. We resent any restrictions or claims put on our way of life in the name of concern for others. They appear to us as intolerable violations of our individual rights. For us there exists only one right: the right to live in peace and not be disturbed. Like Nicodemus, we want to talk about religion but not politics or economics. Let Jesus speak to us about heavenly matters but he had better keep his nose out of our business.

When Robin Roberts received one of the many awards in his long and colorful baseball career, he received it with proper modesty and words to the effect that his real ambition was to get to heaven where the really significant awards would be given. Not only is baseball the great American pastime, his humble acceptance speech illustrates the widespread notion held by many Americans: The purpose of life is to get to heaven and Jesus is supposed to help us get there.

During evangelistic campaigns, posters and bumper stickers are sometimes displayed with the slogan, "Jesus is the answer!" On one such poster someone had penciled in the words, "But what is the question?" For us, Jesus is the one who answers our questions. It never occurs to us that he might just call into question our whole being. But that is just what Jesus does when he warns us to count the cost! It is to us as part of the vast multitude of American seekers after spiritual realities that Jesus speaks. He calls into question our comfortable, self-centered, self-affirming identities and calls us to adopt the values of the crucified one. Unfortunately for Nicodemus and for us, the changes demanded by our confrontation with Jesus are eviscerating. They turn us inside out and demand a whole new identity. Jesus tells us we must be born again! Tinkering around the edges will not do. We must start all over.

The task is to redeem his words. It is not Oral Roberts or Billy Graham speaking. It is Jesus Christ. The Christ who was born for the sake of the oppressed, identified with them even unto death, and who initiated his ministry by claiming, as fulfilled in his presence, the prophecy of Isaiah about preaching good news to the poor, release to the captives and setting at liberty those who are oppressed. It is this bearer of good news to the poor, the captives, and the oppressed who asks over-zealous followers, "Can you drink from the same cup that I do?" It is Jesus Christ who commands, "You must be born again."

When evangelists speak of being "born again" they are talking about a conversion experience. But Jesus was not talking about religion. He was talking about a change of identity: being born again. Starting all over with a radically new persona, an identification with those who are blind or hungry or poor, those in bondage and poverty stricken. Jesus is calling us to make the frustrations of the oppressed our frustrations, their aspirations our aspirations. We are being asked to make their insecurity our insecurity, their struggle our struggle.

"You come to me, Nicodemus, as you are, to talk about heaven and God and I say to you, you must be born again. Are you ready to discount your status, your privilege, your success, to identify with the wretched, the lost, and the damned?" Jesus is not calling us to be his admirers, much less his defenders. He invites us to be followers who are willing to take on the scandal of being born in a barn and the embarrassment of an outcast's cross.

Are we willing to be born again? Are we willing to change our identities? Are we willing to include in our circle of loved ones those who have been condemned to second-class citizenship by our society? Can we abandon the provincialism of "My country, right or wrong; but right or wrong, my country." Can we challenge the assumption that increasing profits for American business is the basic tenet of good global economic theory and practice. Can we deny national security and economic privilege as sacrosanct. "Count the cost," warns Jesus.

Jesus' warning seems dangerously lacking in the popular spirituality of many Christians in this country. The revival of religion among so called "born again Christians," is often nothing more than an emotional jag from which believers escape quite unscathed. Our insurance company executive wants to continue his climb to the top, "I want to stay a businessman, but I want people to know that God changes lives." Perhaps there is no characteristic of Christian faith that is more at odds with current religious trends in this country than Christ's concern for the world's outcasts.

For us as American Christians, Jesus' words cut deep. Our national prosperity and success have made us arrogant. Our arrogance comes from what has come to be called "the Protestant work ethic." Its logic is simple: Since work produces, it is good. And since God likes good people, God rewards those who work. Prosperity is a sign of God's providence and we tip our hat in the direction of the divine every Thanksgiving, by making it a national holiday.

Unfortunately, the logic works in reverse and it is easily concluded that because unemployment does not produce, it is bad. And since God does not like bad people, God punishes those who do not work. The end result is self-righteous arrogance. We can overlook those who live at the margins of our society because they are not worthy of its benefits. Wealth is evidence of God's benevolent approval and poverty is proof of God's righteous indignation. This belief that "good guys win and bad guys lose" has been translated into economic theory in this country with religious fervor. It has become an article of faith in the creed of American Free Enterprise. Bright, ambitious people deserve to be well fed and dressed, while others, who might be classified as "dull" or "lazy," deserve nothing but the crumbs from the blessed table of the prosperous or their discarded clothing offered in charitable rummage sales.

Novac may be right. Capitalism may work because of human sinfulness, but never let us forget that it is human sinfulness and greed that is under the judgment of God.

Our society's obsession with industrial growth and corporate profits raises a moral issue for us. Look through any magazine and feel the energy of the image makers as they proclaim their gospels. As a person we are unacceptable unless we buy Ban deodorant, while Scope mouthwash holds the promise of reconciliation. Unless we buy Scott's Turf Builder and have a greener weed-free lawn we do not really love our neighbor or our neighborhood. Women are not really liberated unless they smoke Virginia Slims and our peace of mind is dependent upon Fixodent that holds our plates firmly in place while we drink our Old Granddad, a sure sign that we are one of the beautiful people. And only if we own a Cadillac can nothing more, nor better, be conceived of in this life.

You may not recognize this person as the image of God but it might pass as a fair reflection of the person in the bathroom mirror. It is the new you, envisaged and molded by a consumer society. All of the advertisements raise a moral issue. Ads do not simply tell us what is available to meet our needs. They are designed to create those needs and sell us goods and services that otherwise we could very well do without. Decisions about dollars is a moral issue because while we are busy buying things we do not need, people are starving to death, dying of disease, living without shelter. Discipleship on Jesus' terms not only nurtures a daring and imaginative social concern, it calls for nothing less than global consciousness.

Given our predilection to read the economic tea leaves as signs of God's pleasure or wrath, we are taken aback when accosted by the words of Jesus. Like Nicodemus, we had hoped to talk about religion, not politics or economics. Our interest in religous revivals and Christ's agenda for disciples are clearly in tension.

To become a disciple of Jesus we have to make a decision involving hard choices. There is nothing automatic about becoming a Christian. We choose to become a follower of Jesus and that decision inevitably involves more than a weekly tip of the hat in God's direction.

For example, our pocketbooks. The privilege of owning private property, and passing wealth on to those whom we designate through inheritance must continually be weighed on the scales of Christian stewardship. Property rights are not articles of faith. Property owners in the Old Testament did not have the right to harvest everything in their fields. They had to leave some of the gleanings for the poor. More significantly, when Israelite farmers purchased land, Levitic law held that they really bought only the use of the land for a period of time until the Jubilee year required its return to the original landowner. The Old Testament ideal of a Jubilee year was intended to provide an institutionalized way of ensuring economic justice in society. It was poor people's right to receive back their inheritance at the time of Jubilee. Returning the land was not a charitable courtesy which the landowners might extend if they were moved to do so. It was a required understanding which was built into the ownership, and, consequently, the stewardship of land.

Similarly, the biblical practice of tithing was the required understanding which accompanied the holding, and, consequently, the stewardship, of wealth. It was not intended as a means of raising money, later to be replaced in the Christian church by the Christmas bazaar or Friday night bingo. It was a structured way to remind owners that all wealth belongs to God.

Tithing is still a useful discipline for believers living in this most affluent nation; believers who are learning to be disciples. Though we may own everything, we are to live as though we possess nothing. The Bible calls us to live as stewards of

79

our possessions rather than owners. Owners develop hardness of heart. Owners develop closed mindedness when it comes to the things of the Spirit. Owners can no longer respond to Christ's invitation to come follow. And churches of owners can no longer offer a Word of hope to the world.

Unfortunately, people on whom lady luck has smiled tend to think the function of government is to protect their property and position. It is not that these folks are any more selfish than others, it is just that people who have been lucky tend to be hard of hearing when Jesus says, "Whoever does not bear his own cross and come after me, cannot be my disciple." We may agree that all of this is very idealistic and impractical, not to mention, "unpatriotic" and inconvenient. We may even reject the terms of discipleship. But we ought not think that we can change them to suit our convenience.

A Seeking Savior

Christian thinking about salvation has divided itself into two main streams which I like to think of as: "Monkey-hold" salvation or "Cat-hold" salvation. The difference in theological viewpoint is seen in how monkeys and cats protect their young. A mother monkey will sound the alarm when danger lurks. The baby monkeys come running to her and hold tightly to her fur as she runs to safety. A mother cat, on the other hand, picks her kittens up by the nape of the neck and carries them in her mouth out of harm's way. So, which is it? Monkey-hold salvation or Cat-hold salvation? Does God sound the alarm in Jesus leaving us to come running and hold on tightly, or does Christ take us by the nape of the neck and carry us to the throne of grace?

At least in these parables it appears to be a Cat-hold salvation. Jesus pictures God as a shepherd who seeks out a lost lamb and carries it home on his shoulders. Or a homemaker who searches every corner of the house for a lost coin until she finds it and rejoices with her friends. Our salvation rests in the care and keeping of a seeking Savior. The message is simple and clear: We do not have to worry about holding on to God's coat tails for God will not let go of ours.

This is what a biblical doctrine of election is all about. Despite what you may have heard or think, the much maligned doctrine of predestination reads something like this: God is so great and good that the Almighty will not entrust something as important as our salvation to someone as unreliable as we. Rather, God entrusts it only to divine care and keeping. The focal point of the Old Testament is the Exodus in

81

which the Hebrew slaves were rescued from their bondage in Egypt. All the credit for their deliverance is given to God who "heard their groaning, and remembered his covenant with Abraham (Exodus 2:24)." In the New Testament, deliverance from sin and death is wrought by Christ. Paul, therefore, his faith fixed firmly on Christ — can boast, "If God be for us, who is against us (Romans 8:31)?"

Predestination is credited to John Calvin, that dour reformer of Geneva. But the idea that God seeks out sinners and takes full responsibility for their salvation did not originate with him. Thomas Aquinas writes of the doctrine. Indeed, long before Calvin was a gleam in his father's eye, Augustine spoke of our election to salvation, as did also the apostle Paul. The doctrine, has of course, raised many questions for logically thinking believers. Yet to deny it, is to deny the biblical God who seeks us out and rescues us from slavery, sin and death. The Negro spiritual has it right, "He's got the whole world in his hands, he's got you and me brother, in his hands!"

To think that our eternal salvation rests with the firmness of our grip on God's coat tails can only give rise to the greatest anxiety. In our saner moments of reflection we know that our grip is weak and unpredictable. Paul speaks for all of us when he cries out in anguish, "I do not do the good I want, but the evil I do not want is what I do. Wretched man that I am! Who will deliver me from this . . . death (Romans 7:19, 24)?" Like a tightrope walker balancing precariously over the abyss, we fear falling and dare not look down. We concentrate so hard on each step that we miss the scenery. There is no good news if our eternal salvation depends upon our grasp of God.

But then the punch line: "Thanks be to God who gives us the victory through our Lord Jesus Christ (1 Corinthians 15:57)." Christ is a seeking Savior! He does not wait for us to come to him!

Dietrich Bonhoeffer speaks of this Savior as God's birthday wish come true. The Holy One's most burning desire was not to remain in heaven with the adoring angels where the latest press clippings and heavenly polls all confirmed the Sovereign's popularity. No, God's birthday wish was to be in and with the world. And, it must be noted, not a world which was sanitized for the divine visitation. There were no secret service agents to "check it out" and make the visit safe. And, clearly, there was no bulletproof limousine to take the expectant couple to the barn. Not a world of antiseptic splendor offering a "red carpet" welcome for prestigious potentates. It was the world you and I see every evening on the nightly news; a world of scandal and dirt, common laborers and corrupt government officials. Yet that is the world God wanted to be with because it beat staying in heaven with all those angels. And his name will be called "Emmanuel," Matthew insists, that is, God with us.

At the root of our word "incarnation" lies the word, "carnal," which the dictionary defines: "In or of the flesh; bodily; material or worldly, not spiritual; having to do with or preoccupied with bodily or sexual pleasures; sensual or sexual." Jesus is God incarnate, that is to say, Jesus is God in carnal form. God's grace is a worldly grace. It is to be understood carnally because that is how it comes to us.

The church has always had trouble accepting that fact. In the early creeds of the church, for example, God was spoken of as having no body, parts or passions. It was offensive to think of a Supreme Being in those terms. Spiritual? Yes! And certainly, heavenly! But theologians have been embarrassed by the frank anthropomorphism of the Old Testament which speaks of God using a body to walk in the garden, smell the incense, and look at rainbows (Genesis 3:8; 8:21; 9:16).

Christian art in the Middle Ages pictured Jesus as a man with a halo adorning his head, all of which obscured the fact that he could command the allegiance of other men, and was physically attractive to women who, the record indicates, flocked around him during his ministry. The church has never had any trouble affirming Jesus as the Son of God with connections in heavenly places, but it has had great difficulty affirming him as a man of the earth, the Son of Man, a title which completely dropped out of use in the early Christian community. Church officials are usually disturbed if ministerial candidates do not confess Jesus as the Son of God, the second person of the Trinity, but seem to care less about insuring the confession that he is the Son of Man.

Historically, this desire to keep Jesus' feet from touching the earth has been labeled the "Docetic heresy." Docetism comes from the Greek word, *dokeo*, which means, "it seems." The heresy believed that Jesus only seemed to be human. In reality, he was eternally divine and had only temporarily assumed a human disguise in order to masquerade among us.

So prevalent was the Docetic heresy in the early church that one of the reasons for the formulation of the Apostles' Creed was to combat its influence. When the Creed affirms that Jesus was, ". . . born of a virgin, suffered under Pontius Pilate, was crucified, dead, and buried. He descended into hell . . . ;" it is attempting to underline with the boldest strokes possible his true worldly humanity: he was born, he hurt, he died, he really was one of us. No masquerade. No pretense. No ifs, ands, or buts about it! He really entered into the human condition to seek and to save the lost.

To say that "God was in Christ reconciling the world to himself (2 Corinthians 5:19)," has less to do with the forgiveness of our sins than with the fact that Jesus did not assume a superior stance with regard to a sin-filled world. Rather, he truly emptied himself and became one of us. ". . . though he was in the form of God, (he) did not count equality with God a thing to be grasped, but emptied himself, taking the form of a servant, being born in the likeness of men . . . he humbled himself and became obedient unto death, even death on a cross (Philippians 2:6-8)."

The descending order from greatness to humility is significant in Paul's letter. Though Jesus was equal with God, he did not count that equality as something to be guarded. Instead he emptied himself, taking on human form. But not just any human form. It was the form of a servant; a servant who was willing to be obedient even unto death. And not just any death! Certainly not the peaceful death of old age after a

84

full life surrounded by admirers. Death on a cross; the ignominious death of a common criminal, deserted and alone. Paul's conclusion is clear: Jesus had no intention of pulling rank. He took off his clerical collar and risked getting decked in the brawl. He risked taking his lumps with the rest of us and in so doing tore down the temple curtain which separated the Holy of Holies from the courts of the profane (cf. Mark 15:38).

Once when flying down to see Grandma, my little daughter asked, as the plane climbed above the cloud castles and broke into radiant sunlight, "Is God up here?" It is a child's question born of a child's understanding of God. Yet many adults never outgrow the conception of God as the Old Man in the sky. When the first Russian cosmonaut returned from his flight into space he tauntingly boasted that he found no trace of God up there. While it is true most thinking Christians would not expect to look for God up — or even out — there, the fact remains that our concept of God presupposes the Holy One is, in one way or another, removed from us and the scenes of our scandalous endeavors.

Luke's gospel offers us no illusions about the waiting world into which Jesus was thrust. Luke begins his gospel by speaking disparagingly of "those days." Those days of Roman rule and oppression, those days of high taxation and hard times, those days when government corruption and the high cost of living were on everyone's mind as they conversed in the market place. Those days when Jewish zealots (that is, terrorists) were plotting the overthrow of the government and hijacking caravans. Those days when life was cheap and public executions — crucifixion-style — were hardly noticed. In those days when the lame and the blind had resigned themselves to their careers of begging, like blind Bartimaeus sitting beside the dusty road going up from Jericho to Jerusalem; when tax collectors like Matthew and Zacchaeus had long since learned that the way to get ahead was to play the game and had willingly sold their souls to the system in order to make a living. In those days when frustrated fishermen like Simon and his brother,

Andrew, had come to the bleak conclusion that the most life could offer them was another day at the nets in their father's boat. In those days, a decree went out from Caesar Augustus that all the world should be enrolled and taxed and taxed and taxed. Now it is precisely at this point that the miracle of the gospel is seen. The claim our faith makes is that it was in a hick town, in those days, in such a place, that the Savior was born, and the new creation of God's kingdom was established. The Savior seeks us, not in the temple courts of the sacred and the sanctified, but in the scandalous world; secular and sinful. The remarkable words of the prophet come to mind, who in announcing the Messianic reign, promised, "... waters shall break forth in the wilderness, and streams in the desert (Isaiah 35:6)." The location of the springs of water and the streams of grace is unimportant. They will break forth in the most unlikely places: the desert wilderness, or in Bethlehem, in "those days."

In Arthur Miller's poignant play, *Death Of A Salesman,* the wife of Willie Loman talks with her son about the father with whom he has become disenchanted. She tries to explain about the man she loves.

> *"I don't say he's a great man. Willie Loman never made a lot of money. His name was never in the paper. He's not the finest character that ever lived. But, he's a human being, and a terrible thing is happening to him. So attention must be paid. He's not to be allowed to fall in his grave like an old dog. Attention, attention must finally be paid to such a person."*[8]

Jesus is God's word that attention has been paid to such a person. God may have other words for other worlds, but his word for this world is "Jesus Christ." It may be true that "Nobody knows the trouble I've seen, nobody knows but Jesus." But he does know. He has been to the front and seen combat. He is Emmanuel — God with us — and Emmanuel is a God who knows what it means to be vulnerable, weak, defenseless. Emmanuel is a God who has joined the troops as a foot soldier slugging it out in the trenches; born in a barn as a helpless babe with the hint of scandal about him and died on the cross a sinner's punishment. If the God of grace be for us, who or what indeed! can be against us. We may be crushed, but we are not destroyed. We may be discouraged, but we are not left in despair. Bereaved, but not reduced to helplessness.

What does it mean to have the Savior seek us and save us? It means our eternal destiny has been decided. Our salvation rests securely in God's care and keeping. We can relax, lift our heads to laugh and sing, and enjoy the scenery.

James Stewart, professor of New Testament studies at the University of Edinburgh, was fond of saying, "Gentleman and ladies, do you realize that one day we will stand in the presence of the angels? And they will gaze in wonder at us and say, 'My, how like Jesus they are!' "

We have God's word on it and that Word has become flesh. "I will not leave you desolate;" Jesus says, "I will come to you . . . because I live, you will live also. In that day you will know that I am in my Father, and you are in me, and I in you (John 14:18-20)." Christ is our guarantee.

Nevertheless, though the new being has been promised, its fulfillment only comes in the "fullness of time." None of us was born suddenly. Our parents may have paced the floor but there was no way to hurry the pregnancy along. Our birth came in God's good time. Similarly, Christ has been conceived within each of us as believers and his birth assured. Still there is no way to hurry the pregnancy along. We can only wait for the birth to come in due time when all will be able to see and admire God's handiwork. Indeed, others may see it long before we are aware of it. The advent of the new being always comes unexpectedly and usually catches us by surprise.

"Nothing is more surprising," says Paul Tillich, "than the rise of the new within ourselves. We do not foresee or observe its growth. We do not try to produce it by the strength of our will, by the power of our emotion, or by

the clarity of our intellect. On the contrary, we feel that by trying to produce it we prevent its coming. By trying, we would produce the old in the power of the old, but not the new in the power of the new. The new being is being born in us, just when we least believe in it. It appears in remote corners of our souls which we have neglected for a long time. It opens up deep levels of our personality which had been shut out by old decisions and old exclusions. It shows a way where there was no way before.'' [9]

When the anguished cry, ''O wretched person that I am. Who will deliver me from this bondage to death?'' has been wrenched from us and we have been forced to kneel mutely before our own inadequacies, trusting the promises of the Savior becomes the only option left to us. Just at the time when it seems as though nothing is happening, when we are discouraged and impatient, just at that time we need to read again these simple stories and discipline ourselves to live as though the leaven is working in the loaf; the new life is being created. Read them again and again, and yet again, because they remind us of the central fact of our existence. We have been sought and found by our Savior!

Proper 20
Pentecost 18
Ordinary Time 25
Luke 16:1-13

Know What Time It Is!

While reading the Bible, Mark Twain once quipped, "It is not the parts of the Scripture that I don't understand that bother me. It's the parts that I do understand." There are plenty of passages of Scripture that speak to us and trouble us. But, alas! for me, this is not one of them. Bernard Anderson referred to the Bible as a special delivery letter with our address on it. That may be true, but this particular bit of Scripture had best be marked, "return to Sender; no one at this address!" This is simply one of those texts that we don't know what to do with. And neither did the early church. They kept adding endings to Jesus' parable trying to make sense of a story that obviously commended the wisdom and resourcefulness of the dishonest steward.

The first attempt is sheer jibberish. "And I tell you, make friends for yourselves by means of unrighteous mammon, so that when it fails they may receive you into the eternal habitations." Can anyone tell me what that means? Taken at face value, Jesus is telling us to buy friends so that when the money runs out these folks will let us into heaven.

The next attempt to vindicate the parable was to tack on some proverbial wisdom: He who is honest can be trusted in all things great and small; but he who is dishonest, cannot be trusted at all. A nice thought, perhaps! But it has nothing whatever to do with the parable. In the parable, Jesus is commending the wisdom of the stewards' ruse, not his honesty.

Things go from bad to worse in the next attempt when we are offered a little moralism to take home with us. "If you have not been faithful in worldly affairs, you will not be trusted

89

with heavenly treasures." Again, probably true. But it totally contradicts the parable.

Not satisfied with any of the above endings, Luke decided to go with a sure-fire winner. Quoting Jesus completely out of context, we read, "No servant can serve two masters; for either he will hate the one and love the other, or he will be devoted to the one and despise the other. You cannot serve God and mammon." Amen!

The music comes up and the curtain goes down. Satisfied that no one is going to argue with that ending, and anxious to get on with it, Luke moves on to other matters.

But what about the original parable? The master commended the resourceful scoundrel when he learned that the day of reckoning was at hand. The point of the parable is that the dishonest steward responded appropriately in light of the impending crisis. Jesus wants us to identify with the scoundrel in the story.

The problem is that we don't like to think of ourselves as scoundrels. Fair enough! But how about sinners? The church calls us "sinners" all the time and we don't seem to mind. Indeed, we own the label quite readily and confess ourselves to be such every Sunday.

One of the basic doctrines of traditional Christianity is that of the atonement. Rooted in the Old Testament sacrificial system, the doctrine holds that God, being holy and perfect, cannot tolerate our sinfulness. Hence we either must not sin — an impossibility if we are to risk living at all — or our sin must be paid for by some sacrifice. It is only when atonement has been made for our sins that pardon can be granted and we are made acceptable in the eyes of God.

Some New Testament writers portray Jesus as the sacrificial lamb who, by his death, procures atonement with God for us (e.g. 1 Peter 1:19 and Revelation 5:12). Jesus, as Savior, sees our sin, is offended by it, and offers himself as a sacrifice for it, thereby obtaining a divine pardon for us. It is across our sinful nature that God in Christ writes the "nevertheless" that makes us acceptable to sacred scrutiny.

But, as Bernard Loomer has pointed out, the problem with sin/forgiveness theology, is that we end up feeling like forgiven sinners.

When Gerald Ford granted a presidential pardon to Richard Nixon, a good deal of discussion resulted both for and against his action. One of the delayed reactions was voiced by former Attorney General John Mitchell who feared that for a pardon to be granted and accepted made the recipient legally guilty. As a result he was concerned that he and the other Watergate defendants would be presumed guilty because of their association with Nixon.

Basic to orthodox theology is the belief that the Almighty is in the business of granting pardons to those who fall short of God's holy will. For nearly 19 centuries the church's faith has operated on the assumption that the essence of the good news is forgiveness. As a result, worship services normally provide for a period of confession during which we acknowledge ourselves as sinners — if not scoundrels — and ask for heavenly mercy. This, in turn, is followed by an assurance of pardon; the affirmation that God mercifully grants us forgiveness.

It is precisely the goodness of such news, however, that is called into question by Nixon's response to the presidential pardon. The fact of the matter is that when the pardon was granted, it had little or no effect on his well being. Gerald Ford may have felt magnanimous in granting the pardon, but Richard Nixon felt guilty and his depression, the reports said, increased.

The problem with this theology for me personally is that while God may forgive me and call me righteous, God does so in spite of who I am. The reality of my being is that I am a sinner. On this point there seems to be little disagreement. God, the Bible, my wife, the neighbors, even my dog; all agree: I am a sinner. Maybe, even a scoundrel. Consequently, God must accept me in spite of myself, but certinly not because of who I am. My being is, therefore, denied at the very center of my existence. In my totality I stand before God as both good and bad. But in the presence of the One who is the Ground

91

of all Being, part of my being is rejected. God grants me a pardon and thereby calls me righteous, but we both know that I am not righteous. I am a sinner, and that fact cannot be changed with smoke and mirrors. I am a mixture of wheat and tares. The Most High may feel righteous in granting me pardon, but I feel forgiven. Instead of feeling free, I feel guilty. I stand acquitted before the jury, but before them I feel awkward and depressed for I know I am, in myself, unacceptable in the eyes of the Judge.

If God is to love us it cannot be in spite of our sin as if it were foreign to our true nature and could be overlooked by Divine benevolence. No! If God is to love us it must be as bonafide sinners. This is where Jesus' parable comes in. He addresses us as scoundrels.

This is not a parable condemning the sinner or his sin. Not only is there no moral judgment implied in the parable, Jesus commends the sinner for his imaginative response to the crisis in which he found himself. Because Jesus believes the kingdom of God is at hand, the point of his parable is: Act appropriately in light of the times. Be as wise as this scoundrel. Know what time it is! Don't just stand there. Do something about it!

But in what sense is the kingdom present in Christ? And how are we to act in light of it?

The kingdom of God has to do with more than merely life after death; the kingdom of Heaven. The kingdom of God is a peculiar perspective on this life; a grace-full view of this sinful world. Consequently, the grace of God has little to do with erasing our sins as if God were shocked by our scandalous lives. Like the cleric who turns red at the telling of a dirty joke we seem to think God is forced to look the other way out of divine embarrassment. Jesus knows all about scandal. He was born in a barn. He died on a cross.

Religious spokespersons contend that we can only begin living when we get our act together, knock off our naughtiness, and begin to love one another. We are told that to be whole we must be holy. The prophets of Madison Avenue have their own version of a sinless society. We must be people with white, sparkling teeth, who smell nice, drive sleek, shiny automobiles on our way to happy homes and prosperous jobs.

But what if in reality our jobs are deadly dull, or we can't get our act together? What if we can't love as we ought and our marriages are on the rocks? Where is wholeness for us if our car is in the garage or the finance company has repossessed it? What if some of our teeth are missing, we sweat a lot, or have bad breath? What does it mean for us, who are sinners, to live with the kingdom at hand?

The reply of the King is, "Take up your cross and follow me."

The cross, let us never forget, symbolizes our sinfulness. The significance of Jesus' reply rests not only on his assumption that each of us has a cross of sinfulness, but more remarkably, that we can bear it. Rather than have us believe we can get rid of our crosses by earnest prayer, positive thinking, or sincere effort, Jesus, who is an expert on crosses, knows that we will not only have to carry our own cross, but that we can carry it. The grace of God is found, not by having crosses miraculously disappear, but in the discovery that we can, in fact, bear them. The Bible is not a book of nursery rhymes in which God is our fairy godmother who waves her magic wand thereby changing pumpkins into royal coaches. Prayers bombarding the throne of grace stemming from that assumption result in frustration if not futility. But the Bible does suggest that behind the scenes stands a grace-full God who offers hope and help for sinners carrying their crosses.

When Jesus as God's anointed King bids us take up our cross and follow him we need to hear his invitation, not as an onerous command to do the distasteful, but as a word of permission to live in our sinful humanity. Furthermore, (and this is the great surprise of the kingdom) the King not only gives us permission to live our lives with all their sinful limitations and weaknesses, but he gives us permission to rename them. We are not locked into the labels that have been assigned us by church or society — "sinner," "scoundrel," "misfit."

Ironically, amazingly, even humorously, Jesus is Savior because the beginning and the ending of his story is cast in scandal. He was born as an illegitimate child. He was crucified as a criminal. The world looks at the life of Jesus with its questionable beginning and sees the cross as its bottom line. By the standards of the world we ought to conclude that he died "prematurely;" that his life began in "scandal" and ended in "failure." He was an "embarrassment" to his family and friends. To his disciples his ministry ended in "tragedy" and "disillusionment." When we are not caught up in a pious sentimentalism we ought to conclude that he was a misfit. The miracle of faith is that we call this misfit, "The Son of God."

Look at how we as believers have come to regard his crucifixion. We call his cross a symbol of "life," not "death." We speak of it as a symbol of "glory," not "scandal." A sign of "hope," not "dead end." "New beginnings," not failure. It is a remarkable feat of faith that we dare to call the Friday of crucifixion, "Good Friday." Jesus' cross is not eradicated, but in the resurrection God gives us permission to rename it. Consequently all of life's "failures" can be seen differently. When we view the scandal of Jesus' life from a divine point of view, we can see the flaws of our own humanity from the same perspective. We are given permission to rename our scandalous lives and experiences gracefully.

The grace of God is like the man who went into the clothing store to buy a suit and was shown a blue one. "No," the customer said, "That won't do. I want a green suit." So the clerk called out to his partner, "Turn on the green light, Joe, the man wants a green suit!" It is not that things are changed. But we see them differently. In Christ we are given spectacles which give us a kingdom perspective. We see ourselves in a heavenly light; through God's eyes. We see how things really are. We need no longer suffer from the stigma that "sinner" — forgiven or otherwise — denotes. We can see ourselves as "heirs" with Christ of the Divine inheritance. The world is not changed, but we see it and ourselves in a new light; a kingdom light.

A Zen story characterizes life as a Buddhist monk fleeing from a hungry tiger. The monk comes to the edge of a cliff cutting off any hope of escape from the pursuing tiger. Fortunately for the monk, a vine happens to be growing over the edge. He grabs hold of it and begins to climb down the cliff, out of the tiger's reach, who is by now glaring at him from above. But alas, as the monk is climbing down, he spies another tiger waiting for him below; circling impatiently at the bottom of the cliff. To make matters worse, out of the corner of his eye he notices a mouse on a ledge above him already beginning to gnaw through the vine. Then out of the corner of his other eye the monk sees a strawberry growing from the rock. So he picks the strawberry and eats it.

Faith in God is not believing that the Holy One will intervene to "save" us. It is knowing what time it is. We live with the reality of sin and death encoded within us, yet we are to live with joy here and now, sinners and scoundrels, because the kingdom is at hand. We are not to demand evidence of its presence. Rather we are to believe it and act accordingly. The claim that we are invited to entertain is that our Savior has overcome the guilt of living and the embarrassment of dying. No longer do we need to apologize for the bumps and warts which inevitably result from living the risk that we call "life." We are not as those who live under sentence of death, but as those who possess the promise of life.

Christian hope is not something we derive from the evidence. Christian hope is something we claim contrary to the evidence and only because the Most High gives us permission through a story to draw contrary conclusions, i.e. to rename the data.

One of the cliches of our culture is that love is blind, but marriage is an eye-opener. Not so! Love sees with amazing clarity; especially if it is divine love. The New Testament Saul had boundless energy and commitment. Unfortunately, he was also hell-bent on persecuting Christians. That is, until he caught God's attention. The Holy One decided that with all that get-up-and-go he would be a good point man for the church. Saul was renamed, "Paul," and the rest is history. Kingdom vision is a perfect 20/20.

Similarly, the Christ of the gospels does not change us, he renames us. That is a crucial distinction. He does not do away with our sinful natures. He simply renames our neuroses and calls them "gifts." Our idiosyncrasies, after all, are what make us interesting. They are what make us unique as individuals. Christ sees them as contributions to life. He does not remove our failures, he calls them "new beginnings." He does not wipe away our mistakes, he says that is how "wisdom" is fashioned. He does not deliver us from our handicaps, he calls them "challenges." And, most assuredly, he does not deliver us from our weaknesses, but rather calls them "strengths" to be shared.

Perhaps the most important gift this parable offers us is the permission to rename our lives because the kingdom has come in Christ. And in so doing, we ourselves are, in some mysterious, even miraculous way, born anew.

Proper 21
Pentecost 19
Ordinary Time 26
Luke 16:19-31

Taking Life Seriously

This parable reminds me of the time I attended an evangelism workshop offered by my denomination and which was intended to demonstrate the latest techniques for saving souls. A team of experts had come to town intent on training us to make cold calls in the community — door to door — seeking converts for Christ. I was assigned to one of the experts as an observer. I was to watch and, thereby, learn the technique. We were armed with two memorized questions which sooner or later were to be introduced into the conversation with our intended converts. The first question to be asked was, "If you were to die tonight are you assured that you would go to heaven?" "Yes," "No," or "I don't know," would suffice as an answer. The second question, however, was the important one, "On what does your assurance rest?" The only acceptable answer was faith in Jesus Christ.

We made our first stop and rang the doorbell. A gracious and charming couple were at home and invited us in. After the pleasantries were exchanged, in which we learned that the husband was a professor of psychology at a large university, I settled back in my chair to observe. I was curious to see how this was going to unfold. Eventually, the first question — the one about dying and going to heaven — was introduced into the conversation. "If you died tonight would you go to heaven?" asked the evangelist.

"I don't know," replied the woman pleasantly, "and we don't really care." This was not one of the rehearsed answers. It fit none of the anticipated categories and pretty well finished the subject. All that was left for the expert to do was either accept the fact that the matter was a dead issue for our hosts

97

or to argue with them, trying to convince them of its importance. In any case, the second question was never asked because there was no way it could be inserted into the conversation. My companion was frustrated and we soon left.

This method of evangelism was based upon the erroneous assumption that heaven is our home and all of us must surely be homesick. Furthermore, we can only get there if we have faith in Jesus Christ. The professor and his wife, however, were focused on life in this world, and the would-be evangelist had nothing to say to someone with no interest in faith or the life hereafter.

The church frequently seems preoccupied with the next life and assumes faith in Christ is required to avoid eternal torment and gain heaven's bliss. Our first reading of this parable, therefore, focuses on the judgment after death. Good guys will win; bad guys will lose! Believers will be rewarded. Nonbelievers will be punished.

But this reading of the parable — like the traditional method of evangelism — misfires on two scores. First, according to the parable, faith in Christ has nothing to do with eternal rewards and punishments. Our destiny is determined, not by our faith in a savior, but by our attitude toward others. The rich man walked past Lazarus every day, but he had no compassion for him. Lazarus' needs were obvious. The rich man felt no sense of obligation in meeting them. It was not his lack of faith in Christ that got his ticket punched, it was his lack of regard for Lazarus.

Second, the parable's focus is on life, not death. As with the professor and his wife, the concern is with this world, not the next. Religion has led us to believe that life in the next world is what really matters. Heaven and hell are where the real action is. Everything else is secondary and preliminary. Our actions here are only of importance insofar as they determine our eternal destiny. We do good in order to get to heaven. As a result, Christian spirituality has often discounted life in this world and those who benefit from our charitable activities become mere pawns in the self-centered game of salvation.

D. H. Lawrence labeled such apparent charity as greedy giving. We are good for ulterior reasons. Life here is only a means to a greater end.

I mean to suggest that the point of the parable is not instruction in how to make it in the next life, but living well in this one. It draws its meaning from the surrounding teachings which make it clear that Jesus wants us to live in this world wisely, responsibly, and charitably. The issues that Jesus sets before us are larger than putting stars in our individual crowns. Human suffering is not a matter of indifference to God. Indeed, it is a matter of eternal importance. God's concern for the well-being of others here on earth follows us to the grave and beyond. Old Jonathon Edwards had it right! In the last analysis a person's business is with God. But God is less concerned with our sinful bumps and warts than with the needs of those around us. The question the Bible continually asks is, "What is the focus of your life?" Do we live for ourselves — our comfort, our security, our salvation — or for others? Micah, the prophet, prompts us with the correct answer. "He has showed you, O man, what is good; and what does the Lord require of you but to do justice, and to love kindness, and to walk humbly with your God (Micah 6:8)." That demand did not change in all the years separating the Old from the New Testaments. Jesus merely gave it visibility and clarity when he told his followers to feed the hungry, visit the prisoner, and clothe the naked. To love God is to love the neighbor. Remember? The eternal question to be asked, here and hereafter, is simply, "How are the neighbors doing?" Their welfare must be of genuine concern to us because it is to God.

So too, the life of our planet earth. Its creation was an act of God. But its destruction could well be our own doing. Polluting the earth with our waste. Cutting down rain forests. Killing off species of wildlife. Punching holes in the protective ozone layer. The photograph of the earth taken from the moon should make it abundantly clear that we are all part of an intricate and delicate ecosystem. This morning as I was putting on my suit, I reached into the breast pocket of the coat and pulled out a slip of paper that read, "This garment has been inspected by number 46." Even the clothes we wear are part of a social network on which we depend.

The question that the parable raises for us is, "What are we going to do with our world? How are we going to shape its history? What legacy do we leave for the neighbors who come after us?" Dietrich Bonhoeffer argues that for Christians the only ethical question is, "How shall the next generation live?" We are stewards of our time and place in history whether we construe it globally or locally. We are responsible for passing history on to someone else. .

The purpose of the parable, then, is to direct our attention to the serious business of living in this world rather than pointing to the next. Indeed, the parable warns about allowing our attention to wander. We do not have all the time in the world to be about it. A sudden turn of events reminds us that we are not eternal. A serious accident. The discovery of a lump while taking a shower. Our lives are bounded by birth and by death — our death. Soren Kirkegaard proclaimed the earnest thought of death to be life's greatest ally. When we begin to do the arithmetic of life, it brings a sense of urgency to take it seriously.

A woman in the hospital was weeping after being told she was terminally ill with cancer. When a friend sought to console her she replied, "I'm not weeping because I'm dying. I'm weeping because I never lived." The awareness of limits and wasted time means we' can take up a conscious stance with regard to our own inevitable mortality. It is this mature insight that will protect us from slavishly following what the culture wants us to do and squandering our time in seeking the approval of others by conforming to their rules and values.

Probably there are no words that control human behavior more than, "What will others think?" We are intimidated by them time and again. Many of us never experience the vast dimensions of our own lives or explore the potential of our capabilities because we are afraid. We are afraid that we are incompetent. We are afraid of ridicule. We are afraid to risk living for fear of what others might think if we fail; so we insulate ourselves from them, clutch our lives and our possessions, and ignore the call to live in the family of humanity. In one of his novels, Nikos Kazantzakis speaks of the American friend of Zorba the Greek. He is reminded over and over of the adventurous life which has eluded him. He is both intrigued and threatened by Zorba's dances in the middle of the night. They lure him to leave the safe havens of prudence and custom in order to depart on great voyages to another world. Yet he is unable to respond. He sits there motionless and shivering. He is ashamed. He has felt this shame before whenever he caught himself not daring to do what supreme recklessness the essence of life called him to do. Yet never did he feel more ashamed than in the presence of Zorba. Ashamed and fearful! Two sides of the same coin.

In my younger days when I was learning to fly I had to practice takeoffs and landings. After one particularly rough landing, something on the order of a controlled crash, I commented ruefully to my instructor, "That was a terrible landing." His reply contained the wisdom of the ages. "It's a good landing if you can walk away from it."

God is not interested in the style of our landings. Onlookers may cluck and comment and roll their eyes. But not God. When we stand before our Creator to render an accounting of our lives, God's concern will not be with our sins and shortcomings. They are foregone conclusions. They are simply part of the cost of living the great adventure. No, God's concern will be with our ability to walk away from the landing with a sense of accomplishment that we have lived well; that we gave it our best shot and tried to leave the place a better world than when we came.

This parable, therefore, reminds us that life is serious business because we have only one life to live; one chance to land. As the selfish rich man woefully found out, there are no second chances. We only have a few years to make this planet a better place; or the life of the neighbor more bearable. We have three score and 10 years, the Psalmist says, or even if by reason of strength (and the luck of the draw) we have four score, yet we are soon gone. We fly away like a sigh. The lesson to be learned is that we need not be actively evil to miss resting in the bosom of Abraham, we need only to be inactively indifferent. We do not have to kick the person who is down; only step over him. We expend our allotment of years for others or we try to preserve them for ourselves. But Jesus warned, "If you save your life, you will lose it. Only if you give it away, will you find it." We can debate the economics or logic of his teaching but we ought to be clear that this is what he believed and taught. It is in this dying-living, living-dying that we find meaning for our lives.

As human beings we can choose how to live and, sometimes, how to die. The cross of Christ reminds us that he chose to die. He was not a victim of circumstances, nor was he a tragic hero. He could have died in bed of old age. But instead, Jesus chose to die. "My hour has not yet come," he kept saying during the days leading up to his final journey to Jerusalem. Finally, during the last meal with his disciples, Jesus uttered the words that must have popped their eyes open, "The hour has come (John 17:1)." The words burst forth, not as a death knell, but the glorious climax to a life intentionally lived. When Jesus invites us to take up our cross and follow him he invites us to live for a cause and die for a reason. We only go around once, and Martin Luther King Jr. put it well when he said, "Until we are willing to die for something, we're not fit to live for anything."

The Christian offers his life for others, not because heaven follows, for that would imply that this life is not as important as the next, but because it is the only opportunity we will have to responsibly live in the time and place in which we have been placed. Kurt Vonnegut has written some superb lines which catch the amazement and delight of life's miracle.

"God made mud . . .
God got lonesome . . .
So God said to some mud, 'Sit up! . . .

See all I've made,' said God, 'the hills,
the sea, the sky, the stars.' . . .
And I was some of the mud that got to sit up
and look around . . .
'Lucky me, lucky mud.' "[10]

But with our lives comes a sense of responsibility for fulfilling the unique opportunity to live them. We realize that no one can do our living or our dying for us. Feelings of inadequacy and guilt inevitably come from trying to live them. Especially when we compare our lives to others or look to external standards of conduct and achievement. "Sin" is a word often used by religious authorities which underscores these feelings. The church frequently plays on our feelings of guilt and fear, using them as leverage to gain conformity. The promise of heaven is used as the carrot. The threat of hell is used as the stick. But it is a sick guilt, and it immobilizes us. It is what Archibald MacLeish calls "the sick scent of dung under our fingernails."

Healthy guilt comes from our failure to discover the miracle of our own unique life and taking it seriously. The cup of opportunity that life hands me to drink is, of course, different from the one that it hands you. Lazarus was not sitting at your door or mine but someone else is! I cannot drink the rich man's cup, but I can drink mine. Indeed, no one can do it for me. True guilt, healthy guilt, motivates us rather than incapacitates us. It comes, not from comparing cups, but from the realization that we have failed to drink the cup that is ours.

"But heaven! What about heaven?" someone is probably asking.

In Jesus' view, heaven is the projection forward, into God's time and space, of a life lived wisely, responsibly, and charitably here. Apparently, self consciousness survives death and we live either with regrets over our lack of responsible stewardship for the years alloted to us, or with joy at new opportunities offered. To be found trustworthy in our custodial responsibilities is to be promoted to larger responsibilities.

103

To whom much is given, much will be expected. The point is graphically made by Jesus in the parable of the talents (Matthew 25:14-30). To one person ten talents are given, to another five, and to another one. The distribution is not equal yet each is expected to invest their resources for the benefit of the landlord. Those who do, are put in charge of greater wealth. The one who fails in his stewardship by hiding his wealth discovers that even that which he has is taken from him. The good news is that if God finds us trustworthy in carrying out the caring concern of the Creator for the planet and its people we are entrusted with even greater responsibilities in the life to come.

More than that we dare not say. It would be nice if we could add, "And they all lived happily ever after." But Jesus — always the realist — was not in the business of telling fairy tales or parables with happy endings. He knew that we live by the choices we make. The ending of the story, therefore, is ours to write. Jesus simply said, "Those who have ears to hear, let them hear!"

Living The Alternatives

"Christ" is the Greek word for Messiah or King. To believe in Jesus Christ, therefore, is to affirm more than certain doctrinal statements about his divinity or the assurance of eternal life. To believe in Christ is to refuse to acknowledge anyone else in this life as King. It is to insist that the powers and principalities of this world do not have authority over us, even when they appear to be in charge. The New Testament writers boldly portray Jesus meeting the powers of this world head on in a showdown. And when it was over and the dust had settled, the resurrection story claims: those powers had been dismantled.

Walter Cronkite used to conclude his summary of the evening news by saying, "And that's the way it is." Political, industrial and religious bureaucrats echo the words, and usually add, "Take it or leave it!" The definers of worldly reality assume they have the right to say how it is, and how it will be. They know who is in charge and everyone else had better know it, too, because that's the way it is.

Unless, of course, you happen to buy the Jesus story. Because, if you do, the gospel newscasters are telling us, "No, that's not the way it is at all! There was this showdown in Jerusalem. Jesus is the Christ, and that's the way it is."

The question before the house is, "Do we believe them?"

When we are completely honest, the answer is probably, "Well, yes; but . . ." So, we, like the disciples before us, cry out, "Lord, increase our faith!" We are fully aware that we need more faith. We have some but it is not nearly enough. Saints have more faith than skeptics, and clearly we want to be on the side of the angels.

105

Furthermore, we assume, as did the disciples, that Jesus is the one to see about increasing our store of faith. They came to Jesus with the request. So do we. His reply to them, as it probably would be to us, is, "If you had faith as a grain of mustard seed, you could say to his sycamine tree, 'Be rooted up, and be planted in the sea,' and it would obey you." Jesus offers, what appears to be, a smart aleck answer. "If you had faith as a grain of mustard seed, you could tell that sycamore tree to move over, and it would do it. If you had even a little faith you could move mountains." In the eyes of Jesus, the disciples apparently had no faith whatsoever! None! Zip! Even a little of it could work wonders, but Jesus says they have not as much as a grain of mustard seed. Evidence: the trees remain rooted.

Can anyone take Jesus seriously? Does any believer truly think that if he or she had enough faith, mountains could be coaxed into leaping around like lambs or trees taken for a stroll? I put it to you that even the most spiritual, deeply committed Christian is doomed to despair if we take the words of Jesus literally. "If between you guys there was enough faith to fill a mustard seed, even that much faith, you could change the landscape," he tells the disciples. Clearly, his reply is at the very least insensitive to their request, not to mention our soul's sincere desire. And at worst, it exhibits callous cynicism.

But Jesus is not one to offer thoughtless answers. That is not his style. So, it is not that he is trying to put his disciples down or make us feel stupid. It is rather that he is cutting off at the pass our assumptions about faith.

Faith does not have to do with God, heaven, or anything else spiritual. On the contrary, faith changes the landscape of this world. It moves mountains and transplants trees. It is not a passport to heaven nor is it a belief about God. Faith is not even belief in God. It is a new understanding of the way this world can be. Faith sees with amazing clarity a reality that others do not yet see.

It was said that the great Michaelangelo attracted a crowd of spectators as he worked. One child in particular was fascinated by the sight of chips flying and the sound of mallet on chisel as the master shaped a large block of white marble. Unable to contain her curiosity, the little girl inquired, "What are you making?" Pausing, he replied, "There is an angel in there and I must set it free."

Faith is seeing the new reality and working to set it free. It is seeing the reality of God's kingdom and working with the Holy One to create the new heaven and earth.

When Jesus insisted, "My kingdom is not of this world," we assumed he was talking about heaven. But, it turns out, faith is a radically imaginative approach to this life. The categories of this world are not finally settled. The definitions that fetter us are not forged in steel. Jesus looks at life from a different and radically imaginative perspective and therein lies the kingdom of God.

Consider, for example, his perception of Zacchaeus, the despised tax collector, who made his living by cheating everyone. When Jesus came to town, Zacchaeus, being very short of stature, decided to climb a tree for a better look. Jesus noticed him out on his limb but the question was, what should he, as Messiah, do? "Try to change Zacchaeus?" the townspeople would have insisted, "You might as well try to turn stones into bread." Those things just do not happen. The options, therefore, were quite clear:

(a) Scold Zacchaeus for being a sinner.

(b) Ignore Zacchaeus because to recognize him in any way gives tacit support to his dishonest dealings.

(c) Laugh at Zacchaeus. He is, after all, a ridiculous spectacle: up a tree.

But Jesus selects a forgotten option: (d) "None of the above." He asks Zacchaeus to come down from the tree and invites himself to Zacchaeus' house for dinner and conversation. The next day the story is flying around town. "Zacchaeus is a changed man. He's not only giving back what he's stolen, but he's giving it back four times over!"

One of the most certain indicators of Jesus' divinity is not his virgin birth, nor his ability to perform miracles. The surest

107

sign that this Jesus is the "Son of the Most High God" is his *modus operandi*, his style; time and again he lives the forgotten alternative.

When faced with the dilemma of 5,000 hungry people late in the day, his disciples came to him with the question, "What shall we do?" Worldly wisdom would suggest:

(a) Tell them to go home.

(b) Tell them to go hungry.

(c) Tell them to get a bite at McDonalds and reconvene at eight o'clock.

Jesus said, "There's another option, (d), 'None of the above.' We will bless what we have and feed them now. We will work with what we have and multiply it."

Christ gives us permission to look at the world differently and, thereby, frees us from the claims and definitions of the reigning authorities. Life is not settled. The way we have been told it is not the way it is at all.

Faith invites us to live with a God who consistently offers other options than those seen by the authorities and power brokers of this world. To those who think that all the categories of life are fixed and the world is a closed system in which there are no surprises, the gospel comes as good news. Faith in Christ brings unexpected alternatives into such an unimaginative world.

So Jesus comes to the poor. The poor, who have long since learned that they have been born poor, they are poor, and they will die poor. Society has defined their possibilities as nil. But Jesus says, "None of the above. Blessed are the poor." And to the meek who know their place in the social pecking order, Jesus turns their understanding of life on its ear by declaring, "Blessed are the meek, for they shall inherit the earth (Matthew 5:5)." To the rich who know what and whom they can buy and sell, who gather for cocktails at the country club while they benefit from the work of others, those who have life under control and know how much is in their pension fund for a secure retirement, Jesus levels the block-buster, "It will be more difficult for you to make it into the kingdom of heaven than for a camel to get through a needle's eye (cf. Matthew 19:24)!" It was not a halo around his head nor a bag of tricks under his toga that caused such commotion among the authorities. It was the way he looked at life. "There's nothing settled about it!" he insisted. "We don't have to grant as final the present situation." Jesus is the Son of God and our Savior because he gives us permission to be in this world, but not of it; not defined by its options, nor bound by its alternatives.

To those who have spiritualized faith by insisting that it has to do with things otherworldly, this parable of Jesus comes as a shock. Faith has to do with this world and seeing it in a different way. There is mounting evidence in the field of cancer research, for example, that faith healing has little to do with belief in God. The research data suggest that patients who are terminally ill have a statistically significant chance of getting well if they can imagine the white blood cells as a victorious army putting to rout the invading army of cancer cells. Faith in Divine providence is not as important as mentally imaging the body as healthy. Faith in this sense is imaginative vision that sees what medical science and others are not yet able to see.

To visualize that which is not, is a uniquely human possibility. Human responsibility — stewardship, if you will — for our planet and our individual lives rests on our capacity for envisioning alternative possibilities to existing realities. That is why it is crucial to be intentional about what we visualize. We are always imagining a future of some sort and letting our lives be shaped by the vision. Faith seeks to fulfill its own prophecy. If we believe that we can be well, our bodies begin to shape themselves around the new vision of health. If we believe that nuclear suicide is inevitable, we and our government, begin consciously or unconsciously, to speed up the process. Faith is simply living as though this is true or that is possible. The object of faith may be a variable, but faith itself, is a unique attribute indigenous to the human enterprise. Faith, in the sense that Jesus spoke of it with his disciples, is simply envisioning and practicing an alternative future. It is daring to risk living by a new vision.

Fortunately, according to Jesus, it does not take much faith to shape a new world. Even a little vision of new possibilities — as small as a grain of mustard — can work wonders. It can uproot trees, transplant mountains, or disarm a nuclear missile in its launch silo. The quantity of faith is not the issue. Apparently a person either has faith-vision or they do not. We either live in a world of possiblities or we live in a world of inevitabilities.

One of the difficulties we encounter in trying to deal with the issues facing our country and the world — unemployment, poverty, human and civil rights, and disarmament, to name only a few — is the paralysis that grips our society. We are overwhelmed and therefore, immobilized by the magnitude of the issues. The public feels powerless. As a result politicians can play on our lethargy and get by with cliches, easy answers, empty promises, and trite solutions. "The issues are too complex," we are told, so we let the "experts" deal with them. But the "experts" frequently do not deal with them and confidence in government "of the people and for the people" has been eroded.

In the face of such hopelessness, the church must call for a miracle of faith. Nothing else can save us. Nothing else can break the bonds of fear and futility. It does not have to be much faith, says Jesus, but it does have to be new. Faith is a new vision.

If mainline churches are languishing today perhaps it is because we have no vision that grips the imagination; one that is compelling enough to command our allegiance and channel our energies. The Old Testament prophets proclaimed the word of the Lord with the wind in their beards and fire in their eyes, convinced that without a vision, the people perish.

When Ezekiel sat in the valley of dried bones contemplating the future of his people, he saw no hope. It was as if the Jewish people had been scattered like so many bones lying bleached in the sun. Not only were they dead, they were scattered. The situation was quite hopeless. In precisely that unlikely cradle, faith was born. The Word of the Lord came to

Ezekiel bringing with it a new vision of the possible. "Behold," God declared, "I will cause breath to enter these bones and they shall live. They shall be joined together and stand before me (cf. Ezekiel 37:1-14)." In the face of such a vision, his feelings of inadequacy and powerlessness were simply luxuries Ezekiel could not afford.

To be made to feel powerless is a satanic trick. We have been duped by bad propaganda if we feel helpless. The parable Jesus gives us makes it clear that any alternative vision can reshape the world, even if it is as small as a grain of mustard seed. To crumble the concrete highway down which our world sweeps with suicidal speed, is to plant the seed of an alternative vision right beside it. In time, the seed will sprout and grow into a mighty tree; its roots reaching and expanding under the road. Eventually the cement will crack and give way to the vitality of its life.

The promise of life contained in that tiny seed is the ground of our hope. It is also a threat because its vitality challenges the powers of death. Faith's vision is destructive as well as creative. There is a dark side to faith. It may be compelling, but it is frightening. It calls on reserves of imagination that see beyond what is. Its vision threatens to disrupt the status quo.

Instinctively we know that the comfort and security of our vested interests are in jeopardy. So we try to ignore it, discredit it, or destroy it. Jesus was not only cruicified as a political threat to the Roman empire, but as a spiritual threat to the religious establishment. Dead, the religious leaders could say what they wanted to about him. Alive, he spoke for himself! Therein lies the danger of a vision. It is like a live grenade rolling around among the troops. You never know when it will go off in someone's imagination. A non-canonical parable makes the point.

Once a farmer sought to raise a single baby eagle which he had found in the wilderness. He raised it with his chickens and it grew strong. But alas! this king of birds came to think of itself as a chicken rather than an eagle. Each day the farmer would throw it into the air hoping to see it fly, and each time it would return to the earth to eat the chicken feed thrown on the ground. One day, however, something began to stir in the bird's memory when it was launched aloft; a strange and fearful excitement surged through its breast. It stretched its wings and soared, lifted by the rising currents of air. The farmer was ecstatic until the eagle, sensing its true nature, swooped down on the chickens in the barnyard, and devoured them.

Faith, in any amount — even as small as a mustard seed — has such carnivorous capabilities because it grips the imagination and calls forth a vision of new possibilities which can destroy the old. Yet, it is the hope of the world. For believers living in, but not of, this world, faith in Christ sees his vision of God's kingdom. We begin to think in alternative terms and dare to live in a new reality; the reality of a new heaven and a new earth.

Footnotes

1. Annie Dillard, *Holy the Firm,* (Harper and Row, 1977), p. 59.

2. Jack Woodard, St. Stephens and the Incarnation Church, Washington, D.C., 1981.

3. Annie Dillard, *Pilgrim at Tinker Creek,* (Bantam Books, 1974), pp. 15ff.

4. Paul Tillich, *The Shaking of the Foundations,* (Charles Scribner, 1948), pp. 149-150.

5. Lowell D. Streiker, *The Promise of Buber,* (J. B. Lippincott, 1969), pp. 13-14.

6. Mary Caroline Richards, *Centering on Pottery, Poetry, and the Person,* (Wesleyan University Press, 1964), p. 27.

7. Michael Novak, "A Closet Capitalist Confesses," *Wall Street Journal,* April 20, 1976, p. 2.

8. Arthur Miller, *Death of a Salesman,* (Penguin Books, 1976), p. 56.

9. Paul Tillich, *The Shaking of the Foundations,* (Charles Scribner, 1948), p. 182.

10. Kurt J. Vonnegut, *Cat's Cradle,* (Dell Books, 1963), p. 149.

Lectionary Preaching After Pentecost

Virtually all pastors who make use of the sermons in this book will find their worship life and planning shaped by one of two lectionary series. Most mainline Protestant denominations, along with clergy of the Roman Catholic Church, have now approved — either for provisional or official use — the three-year Common (Consensus) Lectionary. This family of denominations includes United Methodist, Presbyterian, United Church of Christ and Disciples of Christ.

Lutherans and Roman Catholics, while testing the Common Lectionary on a limited basis at present, follow their own three-year cycle of texts. While there are divergences between the Common and Lutheran/Roman Catholic systems, the gospel texts show striking parallels, with few text selections evidencing significant differences. Nearly all the gospel texts included in this book will, therefore, be applicable to worship and preaching planning for clergy following either lectionary.

A significant divergence does occur, however, in the method by which specific gospel texts are assigned to specific calendar days. The Common and Roman Catholic Lectionaries accomplish this by counting backwards from Christ the King (Last Sunday after Pentecost), discarding "extra" texts from the front of the list: Lutherans follow the opposite pattern, counting forward from The Holy Trinity, discarding "extra" texts at the end of the list.

The following index will aid the user of this book in matching the correct text to the correct Sunday during the Pentecost portion of the church year.

(Fixed dates do not pertain to Lutheran Lectionary)

Fixed Date Lectionaries *Common and Roman Catholic*	Lutheran Lectionary *Lutheran*
The Day of Pentecost	The Day of Pentecost
The Holy Trinity	The Holy Trinity
May 29-June 4 — Proper 4, Ordinary Time 9	Pentecost 2
June 5-11 — Proper 5, Ordinary Time 10	Pentecost 3
June 12-18 — Proper 6, Ordinary Time 11	Pentecost 4
June 19-25 — Proper 7, Ordinary Time 12	Pentecost 5
June 26-July 2 — Proper 8, Ordinary Time 13	Pentecost 6

114

July 3-9 — Proper 9, Ordinary Time 14	Pentecost 7
July 10-16 — Proper 10, Ordinary Time 15	Pentecost 8
July 17-23 — Proper 11, Ordinary Time 16	Pentecost 9
July 24-30 — Proper 12, Ordinary Time 17	Pentecost 10
July 31-Aug. 6 — Proper 13, Ordinary Time 18	Pentecost 11
Aug. 7-13 — Proper 14, Ordinary Time 19	Pentecost 12
Aug. 14-20 — Proper 15, Ordinary Time 20	Pentecost 13
Aug. 21-27 — Proper 16, Ordinary Time 21	Pentecost 14
Aug. 28-Sept. 3 — Proper 17, Ordinary Time 22	Pentecost 15
Sept. 4-10 — Proper 18, Ordinary Time 23	Pentecost 16
Sept. 11-17 — Proper 19, Ordinary Time 24	Pentecost 17
Sept. 18-24 — Proper 20, Ordinary Time 25	Pentecost 18
Sept. 25-Oct. 1 — Proper 21, Ordinary Time 26	Pentecost 19
Oct. 2-8 — Proper 22, Ordinary Time 27	Pentecost 20
Oct. 9-15 — Proper 23, Ordinary Time 28	Pentecost 21
Oct. 16-22 — Proper 24, Ordinary Time 29	Pentecost 22
Oct. 23-29 — Proper 25, Ordinary Time 30	Pentecost 23
Oct. 30-Nov. 5 — Proper 26, Ordinary Time 31	Pentecost 24
Nov. 6-12 — Proper 27, Ordinary Time 32	Pentecost 25
Nov. 13-19 — Proper 28, Ordinary Time 33	Pentecost 26 Pentecost 27
Nov. 20-26 — Christ the King	Christ the King

Reformation Day (or last Sunday in October) is October 31 (Common, Lutheran)

All Saints' Day (or first Sunday in November) is November 1 (Common, Lutheran, Roman Catholic)